THE
CLIMB
OF YOUR LIFE

Dan Miears

Wasteland Press
www.wastelandpress.net
Shelbyville, KY USA

The Climb of Your Life
by Dan Miears

Edited by Carol Lindsey

Second Printing – October 2014
ISBN: 978-1-60047-851-2
Library of Congress Control Number: 2013935295

Printed in the U.S.A.

0   1   2   3   4   5

DEDICATION

I would like to dedicate this book to my family and friends who have always supported me and my dreams.

To my beautiful wife Crissie: You are the fuel that inspires me to higher ground in my daily climb. I appreciate you sticking with me through the good times and the bad. I hope that we have learned much from the joys and sadness we have been confronted with and embrace the life we have with boundless energy to make the most of each day.

To my children, John and Emily: You are the reason that I work so hard and push myself to my greatest potential. This book is written for you. I hope that, long after my time on this Earth is done, you and your children will enjoy and benefit from the contents of this book.

To my parents, all of them: I have been blessed to have the best parents a child could want for. To my mom, who has endured much in her lifetime; that she may find joy in the life her children live and that her love and sacrifice for me and my brother was not wasted. To my dad and stepmom, Caren; thank you for always being there and giving me support and encouragement along the way.

To Clarence and Helen; there are no greater in-laws one could ask for. Your genuine kindness and caring of others has always inspired me to do the same.

To My Brother Joe: We have seen more than our fair share of difficulties in our lives. We continue to endure the changes and live each day as best we can. You have always been my best friend.

To Kenn and Cyndi: We have lived so much of our lives sharing the joy of bringing our beautiful children into this world, raising them, showing the importance of family and being there for each other. I love you both as if we were my brother and sister.

I would like to thank my son John Wallace Miears II for this drawing that was the inspiration for the cover of the book.

FOREWORD

The *Climb of Your Life* is a humorously written account of Dan Miears' realization of Anne Frank's statement that "The final forming of a person's character is in their own hands." On September 8, 1989, Dan, age 30, was working, married, and was to become a dad. Going for a motorcycle ride with his dad that day ended by his careening off a mountain road and falling eighty to ninety feet into some trees. As a result, Dan sustained more injuries to his body than one person should ever have, resulting in almost losing his life.

When I met Dan as his physician about a month post accident, Dan was sick, had a mild brain injury, had a fractured leg and had a complete spinal cord injury at his mid chest, so no leg movement. Henry David Thoreau said "Things do not change, we do". Dan had to change day by day as he progressed through rehabilitation. In Dan's accounting of his "climb back", a request by his recreational therapist, which probably seemed strange at the time, actually forecast the way Dan would perform successfully in his quest for a new life. This read is his story and the lessons can be applied to anyone's growth and development.

David F. Apple, Jr., MD
Medical Director Emeritus
Shepherd Center

During the writing of this book I had the opportunity to meet Henry Winkler at a function at Shepherd Center. He's best known as, "The Fonz," on the classic television show Happy Days. Henry is also a very successful co-author, with Lin Oliver, of a series of books about an imaginative, dyslexic fourth-grader named Hank Zipzer. He gave me some very helpful advice as an author which I have used as a foundation in the writing of this book. Thanks Henry for the suggestions you gave me.

CONTENTS

AUTHOR'S INTRODUCTION

"Every man dies. Not every man really lives."
- William Wallace, from the movie Braveheart

I have given presentations to thousands of people over the years and have been asked numerous times if I had a book, a video, something that the audience members could share with others they know who could benefit from hearing my words of wisdom and encouragement. For many years, I have collected my observations and the inspirations of others and put most of them in the book you are about to read. I hope that you will find it just as inspirational and motivational as the audiences that I've had the opportunity to speak to.

It's my belief that most people will go through life never knowing what their true capability is or discovering what gifts they have that are truly unique to them. Most people's lives resemble a rut in the road that I call their daily life. This rut essentially is the route they travel to work, to events and activities that make up their life. This rut could've been by their own design or the design of others that they just fell into and took as their own. They go through their daily routine seeing the same people, doing the same things with little chance of spontaneous change in course or direction. My hope is, after reading this book, you will get out of your rut and discover that the world is once again a flat surface and you can go any direction you want.

The most valuable things you possess in life are the things that you have worked the hardest to obtain. "The Climb of Your Life" is to reach your own summit, a journey that, if taken to its potential, will consume all of your effort and energy. You will have gone farther and done more than you could've ever imagined. "The Climb of Your Life" is one of self-discovery. If you have ever lived your life at all you have seen joy and sorrow almost on a daily basis. Ultimately, your "life's climb" is the culmination of the effort you put into your life, the attitude you approach life with, and how you respond to the events that occur in your life.

This book is a gut check for where you currently are in your own "life's climb" and will re-energize you to focus and aim for higher ground. Are you ready to begin? Good - let's go!

CHAPTER ONE:
Two Climbs in Life

"A man does not climb a mountain without bringing some of it away with him, and leaving something of himself upon it."
– Sir Martin Conway

There are two possible climbs you will face in life: the easy climb and the ultimate climb. The easy climb is the one most taken, because it requires the least amount of effort and attention. The ultimate climb is the constant pursuit of obtaining higher ground and getting to the summit, the highest point attainable in your life's journey.

An example of an easy climb is Stone Mountain, located near Atlanta, Georgia. Stone Mountain is a very well-known granite rock hill. At its summit, the elevation is 1,686 feet above sea level and 825 feet above the surrounding area. The summit of the mountain can be reached only by a walk-up trail on the west side of the mountain, or by a sky lift. The walk to the top can be done in thirty minutes to an hour, depending on your pace.

In contrast, Mount Everest, the world's tallest peak, is the "ultimate climb". I'm sure you have seen movies and heard many stories regarding the attempts to climb

Mount Everest. Mount Everest, a part of the Himalayan mountain range along the border of Nepal and Tibet, is the world's highest peak at 29,029 feet. There are many obstacles in climbing Mount Everest. There is only one third of the oxygen in the air as there is at sea level. At the summit, the temperature can be 100° below zero but most of the climbers can expect around 15° below zero. The cost to be part of an expedition can be in the tens of thousands of dollars. It can sometimes take years of preparation to attempt to climb the summit and it is virtually impossible to do it alone. Some have attempted it with very little training, relying on luck and the help of their guides to get them to the summit.

The first time the summit was successfully reached was on May 29, 1953 when Sir Edmund Hillary, with the help of Tenzing Norgay, a Sherpa out of Nepal, climbed to the summit via the southeast ridge route. Sherpas are often from the Kumbo village and are typically employed as guides. They are highly regarded as elite mountaineers and experts in their local terrain, assisting their clients to get to higher ground and, ultimately, attempt to reach the summit. This takes acclimatization at the base camp and the other four camps before the last climb to the summit.

As of the writing of this book, approximately 4,000 people have attempted to climb Mount Everest. Of that number, only 660 people have successfully reached the summit. There have been 142 reported deaths of climbers during that time. Most would agree that without the help of Sherpas, they would never have made it to the summit or back to base camp.

In your own "life's climb", you cannot reach your summit without the help of many Sherpas along the way. Without them and without a team behind you, the climb would not only be more treacherous, but you would also find it hard to get or stay motivated to keep climbing. Most people will fail in reaching their summit because they quit or give up! The climb is too much! They never reach their own summit, the peak of their own "life's climb".

CHAPTER TWO:
My Own Life's Climb

"Never forget that life can only be nobly inspired and rightly lived if you take it, bravely and gallantly, as a splendid adventure in which you are setting out into an unknown country, to face many a danger, to meet many a joy, to find many a comrade, to win and lose many a battle."
- Annie Besant

I was born in a small town in Texas in 1959 and was the second child of a young mother who had to marry early in life. At 15 years of age, her personal "life's climb" was interrupted when she married someone much older than she who promised to take care of her mom. Her mom needed surgery to save her life and he offered to pay for it in return for her hand in marriage. My mom's life, to that point, had already had many challenges and struggles to get ahead. She was one of three children born in a poor household that offered little assistance in her becoming an adult. My mom, being a fighter, always reached out to others in the community for the guidance and support that was so lacking in her home life.

After marrying my father, my mom went on to have four children; my brother Joe when she was 16, me when she was 17, Kelly when she was 18 (who sadly passed away shortly after birth), and my brother Timmy (who later passed away when he was three with an in-operable brain tumor)when she was 20 years old. My father, as it turned out, wasn't much of father figure. He liked to gamble and drink a lot. My mom finally had enough and we moved back to live with her mom in Kerrville, Texas. I don't recall really missing my dad after that. I guess there weren't a lot of memories to hold on to.

His mom, Marie Waddell, though, lived on a farm outside San Antonio. She was a blast. We would go stay with her and loved every minute of it. She always had a board game for us to play and let us watch the black-and-white TV in her living room. I remember watching "Rat Patrol" and playing with my G.I. Joes ®. As I found out later, during World War II, she worked at the airplane assembly plant there in San Antonio. She was a "Rosie the Riveter" attaching the panels inside the plane's wings every day.

Her husband, Grandpa Pete, had passed away. I don't recall too much about him, but I do remember going to their farm often. There were many farm animals there including, Bingo, a horse I claimed as my own. Grandma Marie had a Dachshund that we named Butch.

We found out later Butch was a female when she started having puppies. We didn't know the difference between boy and girl dogs and she was called Butch the rest of her life. There was always mischief that my brother and I would get into when we visited. After Grandpa Pete passed away, Grandma Marie raised cattle

to make enough money for a down payment on a home and moved to San Antonio.

Living with my mom's mother, Grandma Waite, and her husband, Richard, was a mixed blessing. She was mean as a snake and I am not really sure that she ever really liked children. My mom went to work at J C Penney in town and my grandmother would babysit my brother and me during the day.

She never really liked cooking and one day she asked my brother and me what we would like to have for lunch. We said fried chicken, mashed potatoes, and gravy. Well, she set out to get us good, and told us to go out to the chicken house and each kill a chicken. She didn't tell us how to kill the chicken, so my brother and I improvised as best we could. He grabbed a sharp knife and I, evidently, grabbed a butter knife and headed out to the chicken coop. We really didn't know how to kill a chicken, so we thought the best thing to do was to cut its head off. Of course we had to catch the chicken first, which was quite a feat. I think my chicken just gave up because after catching it, I was having no luck at all with the butter knife. My brother had already made quick work of dispatching his chicken on to the next world. We asked my grandmother what to do next and she said we had to take the feathers off. Once again, she didn't tell us how to do it. Somehow we removed most of the feathers and went back to my grandmother and asked what to do next. She said we had to open up the belly and pull out all the innards (we had no idea what innards were). My brother let me borrow his sharp knife and together we figured out what to do and once again went back to my grandmother for advice. She said, of course, we had to cut it up into pieces but, once again, she didn't tell us how. This game of hers went on for what seemed like hours and, after cutting up the pieces, I think I ended up with five or six. She prepared the grease and told us to dredge the pieces in milk and flour, whatever that meant, and she would fry it for us. The potatoes were as big a fiasco, as we had no idea what we were doing. I'm not even sure if she cooked my chicken all the way but, needless to say, my brother and I never asked what was for lunch anymore and tried to eat whatever she made.

One thing that she did let us do during nap time was sleep on her bed, as she had the only fan in the house. This was probably more for her benefit than ours. I now can understand how difficult my mom's childhood must have been living with grandma. To think mom gave up her teenage life and dreams to marry a man she didn't know, to save her mother's life. Wow.

My Grandpa Richard was a really nice man. He worked at a gas station and when he came home after work he, usually, brought my brother and me a small treat from the vending machine. He always seemed to have calmness about him that made being with my grandmother tolerable.

I was a goofy looking kid at that time, with big ears and pigeon toes (my mom said that let me run faster). I was made fun of a lot back then and, fortunately, as you get older, you seem to remember less and less of the taunting. My brother and I were in the newspaper one time holding Troll Doll® toys that had just come out. In the picture, I believe I was uglier than the troll doll, no front teeth, a crew cut and big ears. I'm sure I helped sell a lot of Troll Dolls® after people saw that, (ha, ha).

My mom worked very hard at J C Penney and would also do illustrations for the store's newspaper ads since, at that time, the local newspaper didn't use photos of clothes in their ads very often. I would later find out that she had taken a correspondence course for artists through the mail and actually had a letter signed by Norman Rockwell who critiqued one of her submissions. They were great illustrations and my mom always had a great flair and creativity with her art.

We were cramped with all three of us living in one bedroom and my mom finally found a house on Lake Ingram she could afford that rented for $50 a month. It was a small place that overlooked the lake and Ingram Dam.

My brother and I started going to a new school with grades 1 through 12 in the same building. I remember getting on the bus very early every morning and taking forever to get to school. We had a great time, though, living across from the lake. My brother and I stayed by ourselves often, and as you can imagine, were very mischievous in the activities we came up with. We did everything from shooting at each other with our BB guns, to sliding to the bottom of the backside of the dam on drainage boards.

I remember one time my brother and I decided to surprise everyone with a Christmas tree and we took the bow saw and headed out into the woods. After cutting the tree down and dragging it home, we realized that the base of the tree would not fit into the holder, so we made the decision to cut it down to a smaller diameter. My brother said he would hold the base of the tree while I cut it off with the saw. This was not a wise move. I skipped the saw off the trunk of the tree straight across his hand and he immediately started bleeding - a lot. We both panicked and he took off running, leaving a trail of blood through the house to the closet that he had gone to hide in. It didn't take long for my mom to find him, following his trail from the scene of the crime. He needed to go to the emergency room and received stitches as a permanent reminder of our first Christmas tree expedition. We got into a lot of trouble after that and there were many other adventures we conjured up and explored.

Time went by and my mom met and started dating John Miears, a towering man who worked in the medical diagnostics field. Shortly after, they were married and we relocated to Houston, Texas. We lived in Houston for little over a year, as I recall.

In 1970, we moved once again, this time to Atlanta, Georgia. It took some time for me to start calling John "dad", since I wasn't really sure what calling him dad would mean, but for me, I had a man that I could respect and look up to and, as awkward as the first time calling him dad was, it meant something to me.

Coming to Georgia was another adventure in a long line of adventures and new schools. By that time, my brother and I had already changed schools many times and friends as well.

The school system in Georgia was much different than what we had experienced in Texas. Come to find out I wasn't very smart at all. In fact, I had to take remedial classes to get caught up with my classmates. I had a difficult time committing myself to understanding what I was learning and applying it to my life at the time.

I had always been somewhat shy in school and, although I had a lot of friends, my brother was still my best friend. While I was still shy with girls, he seemed to have already figured them out. Going steady and giving a girl a bracelet seemed to be the epitome of the boy-girl relationship.

When my brother and I were 12 and 13, John, who I now considered to be "my real dad", adopted us and our last name was changed from Crawford to Miears. Although my dad traveled a lot during the week, he was home on the weekends. He was often put into the precarious scenario of, *"wait till your father gets home"*. So my dad would get home on the weekend and have to put on "the bad cop" uniform. Later, I realized that this was very unfair to him. My brother and I took advantage of my mom during the week and he would have to give most of the discipline when he got home.

By the time we reached high school, Joe was well on his way to being a *"big man on campus"* and I was more known as Joe's brother. I did make some great friends in high school that I'm still close to today, Ralph and Mike. We were not part of the in crowd, but could hold our own if needed.

As far as school work went, I often put as little effort as possible into it and got out of it just what I deserved. I took Latin I think, mostly just to annoy the teacher, Mr. LaDuca. He was a short, pudgy man from New York. He once made me stand up in class, I was much taller than he, and accused me of being a "dad ratted communist" for not doing my homework. I never quite knew where that comment came from, but I still find it somewhat humorous even now.

My mom had visions of me being a doctor, so I took biology. The teacher, Ms. Burke, asked me why I was in the class since I was failing and didn't really get it. I didn't have a good answer and telling her that my mom wanted me to be a doctor and I needed to take this class to fulfill my mom's dream didn't seem like the right thing to say at the time. I wasn't a renegade in school, I just had no dream of my own to pursue and the academics of high school didn't provide me with any direction.

When it came time to get my driver's license, I had no car of my own and had to take my driving test in my dad's company car. Somehow I passed and now needed to work on getting something to drive. My brother was driving a 1964 Mustang that my dad had restored. I was working at Northlake Mall at the time, helping put up displays and other odds and ends inside the mall. I was making minimum wage at $3 per hour and working part time. It was going to have to be a very cheap car.

Rick Hewitt's dad, a friend of mine down the street, owned Checker Cab Company in Atlanta. Rick's dad said that he could get me one of the older cabs that had been retired for a cheap price. So, for $100 I bought a 1967 Plymouth Fury III that needed a transmission. I went out to R&R Auto Salvage on Buford Highway and bought a used transmission for $100 and had it installed for $60. This thing was a behemoth of a car. I could have put six friends in the trunk and sneaked them into the drive-in theater, and the backseat could've passed as a living room. The air conditioner ran cold, the engine ran rough, but it was all mine.

Unfortunately, the engine had a short life and my dad borrowed it one time and the engine locked up on him. Since my brother got to drive the Mustang, there may have been some guilt that my parents felt and my dad

went shopping for
another car for me.
There was a
Chevron station
near Tucker High
School that sold
used vehicles. I

went with my dad to see what they had and the choices
were a blue AMC Pacer with Navajo print interior and
three-on-the-tree manual transmission or a white Gremlin
with a red racing stripe, black vinyl interior and no air
conditioning.

A decision was made to buy the Gremlin. If you ever
want to know what abstinence looks like in an
automobile, the Gremlin is it. For all you parents out there
that are reading this and want to protect the virginity of
your child about ready to get their driver's license and
start driving, then get them the ugliest car you can find.
It's no guarantee, but at least, for boys, it does limit their
attraction from the opposite sex.

I did have relationships in high school, mostly dating
girls from other high schools nearby. As Homecoming
Dance and Senior Prom came around, I often scrambled
to find someone who would go with me. Maybe I was just
an awkward, goofy kid who wasn't mature enough for
serious dating. That, combined with the Gremlin, assured
that my virginity remained intact throughout my senior
year.

Sadly, after graduation my parents got a divorce. This
was a very difficult time for me. I loved both of 75ithem

very much and what went on in their relationship, I felt, should not have impacted the relationship that I had with them. This has always been a point of contention for me as I have moved through my adult life. Keeping my relationship intact with both parents and not really saying too much about either one of them in front of the other one. Both my parents would later remarry and this expanded the number of parents in my life.

After graduation, my brother was off to Tulsa, Oklahoma on a football scholarship. Most of my classmates went off to college and I went to work at a neighbor's business in Tucker that manufactured screens and storm windows. I had worked for them during the previous summer and on weekends. It was a lot of repetitious work and didn't pay very well. The people I worked with were very hard workers and, for the most part, content with the work they had. I guess life had not created a lot of opportunities for them and this would be the type of work they would probably do the rest of their lives. I started to realize that if I didn't do something different, this could be where I would end up in life as well.

Later on, I went to work at a Shell gas station and started attending community college at the insistence of my mother. All of the goofing off and not knowing the importance of good grades and doing well in high school limited my options for continuing my education. I had no idea what I wanted to do; therefore, I had no idea what I needed to do to get ahead in life. This is one of the greatest mistakes most kids make while they're in school.

Looking back, I don't believe you need to know what you want to do, you just need to know whatever you're currently doing, do your best and the rest will, hopefully, be found out later.

I soon realized that girls often liked guys more that knew how to dance. At that time, disco was still very popular, so I learned how to dance hoping girls might find me more attractive. I got good enough to win some dance contests around Atlanta and had a contract to teach dancing at My Fair Lady Fitness Centers in the Atlanta area. I learned a lot about relationships with women, and had some great dance partners to work with.

My friend Mike and I had the opportunity to move to Destin, Florida and stay with some good friends of his dad's, Bill and Babs Burleson. So, I loaded up my Gremlin and,

with $50, headed to the beach not knowing what I would do for work once we got there. I hoped that I would be doing something. Bill and Babs were very gracious in taking us into their home - really their guest house, which was an old travel trailer that was 20 feet long and 6 feet wide and 6'6" tall. Mike and I were both approximately 6'5" tall. It was tight quarters, but it was a free roof over our heads while we worked on our plan of attack to take over Destin.

I had several odd jobs ranging from weeding rich people's gardens, to stocking the shelves at the Jitney Jungle Supermarket, to bussing tables at La Fountain's Wharf restaurant. We both eventually went to work for a taxidermist. We did mostly the grunt jobs that no one else wanted to do. It was very interesting learning how to do skin mounts of animals and fish. We would eventually travel to several Fishing Tournaments to collect Blue Marlin and other large trophy fish that people wanted mounted.

At night, Mike and I would hit the bars in Destin and Fort Walton Beach. We would try and impress the ladies with our dance moves and, overall, had a great time. We ended up renting a trailer near the Okaloosa Bridge for the summer. Ralph came down and joined us for a week and his parents thought we had kidnapped him and he wouldn't be returning home. Mike and I had a great time in Destin. As fall rolled around, it was time to go back to Atlanta and figure out what to do next.

Mike and I would eventually hook back up, working for a small landscaping company that had recently started. We mostly did commercial work for apartment complexes, Hardee's, and Del Taco restaurants.

So, the shy guy with long hair and a Gremlin had an epiphany. If I ever was to get over being shy and build my self-confidence, I should go into sales and force myself to talk to people and try to make a living doing it. I attended a seminar that touted the opportunity of a lifetime selling outdoor electrical signs to small businesses on straight commission.

The company was American Display Incorporated, out of Tustin, California. I learned a lot working with them but realized that I was not going to make the tremendous amount of money that I was led to believe I would. There was a canned sales pitch that we were to learn and develop "one call closing" techniques that were to generate sales on a daily basis. So once again, my trusty Gremlin and I went off on another adventure. Keep in mind, the Gremlin did not have air conditioning and, with the black vinyl interior, the car was always scorching hot during the summer time, which always seemed to be the time that I went off on these new adventures. After traveling around with other salespeople and not making as much money as I had been led to believe, I gave up my traveling sideshow and looked for meaningful work once more.

After several retail sales positions, including managing a men's clothing store and a waterbed and mattress store, I ended up at Seay's Home Furnishings. Not too long after I started working there, Seay's was bought out by Rhodes Furniture. During the "Going out of Business Sale", I was approached by a customer whom I worked with to apply for an outside sales position with a picture frame molding manufacturer and importer, Eric Schuster Incorporated, in Paramus, New Jersey. I went through training at the home office in New Jersey and relocated to Houston, Texas.

This was in the mid-80s when Texas was still recovering from the oil bust. My territory was coastal Texas and the state of Louisiana. Business was slow but I had a great time. On a visit back to Atlanta, I attended my brother's company party for Roberds Furniture and Appliances. I was introduced to one of his co-workers, a young attractive blonde who worked in the office, Crissie Bradberry. I was only at the party for a short while because I had to catch the redeye flight back to Houston.

Several months later I moved back to Atlanta and moved in with my brother. It wasn't too much later that I had the opportunity to run into Crissie again at another Roberds party. She looked as attractive as before. She was six years younger than me which I joked with her about as we talked into the evening. We started to date, nothing serious at first, but as time went on, I discovered she was the one for me!

After looking at several sales positions, I went to work for The Pacesetter Corporation as a salesperson, a window and door manufacturer. It was a straight commission job selling residential home improvements. I started to get pretty good at it and began winning quarterly trips and other monthly incentives and prizes.

In 1987, after living together for a while and living in sin in the eyes of some, I asked her to marry me. My wife will tell you it was not one of the most romantic proposals. We were leaving a bar on Pleasant Hill Road and, as we were walking to the car, I said, "Well we should probably go ahead and get married". It was not the proposal that I had in mind but, nevertheless, it was heartfelt. We had a nice wedding in a small church in Lawrenceville, Georgia, her hometown.

CHAPTER THREE:
Roadside Memorials: Marking Journeys Never Completed

Dan Miears Sept. 8, 1989

"The road of life twists and turns and no two directions are ever the same. Yet our lessons come from the journey, not the destination."
– Don Williams Jr.

Roadside memorials mark the journey of someone's last moment alive on this earth. All of their gifts, love for friends and family ended right there. For me, if it had not been for my dad, a roadside memorial with my name on it would have been placed on the highway in remembrance of me.

The accident itself, in my dad's words:

I remember how the trip that Dan and I were taking all began. Caren and I were over at Dan and Crissie's apartment. It came up that I was going to take a couple of days and go to the mountains on my bike and camp out. Dan said that sounded like a great idea, and said he would like to do that sometime. Caren reminded me that I had a second bike and he should go with me. I wondered why I had not suggested that instead of leaving it up to her to always come up with the good ideas. It was settled. We were going on a father-son camping trip.

The next weekend, Dan came over early and we loaded up the bikes with sleeping bags and a tent, and we were off to the mountains.

Everything was going along fine until we got on Hwy. 400, and I noticed that the headlight on Dan's bike was not working. We pulled over to the side of the road to check it out. It is dangerous, as well as against the law to operate a bike without proper lights. After a few minutes, I found a fuse that had come lose, and the problem was corrected.

We continued on and soon had gone past Dahlonega, and started up Hwy. 19 towards Blairsville. Everything was going fine, and we were headed uphill and had a double lane on our side of the road. I went around a truck, and, as I completed the pass, I checked my mirror to be sure Dan had also passed. I couldn't believe what I saw. It looked to me as though Dan had gone past the truck, but then went straight ahead instead of completing the turn. I stopped in the middle of the road, hoping I was wrong, and that I would see him come around the bend. When he didn't, I panicked, tried to make a sharp U-turn on the sloped road and dropped my bike. I just left it where it fell and started running back down the highway. The first thing I saw was the truck stopped on the side of the road, and three men staring down into a steep gorge.

There was the bike with the entire front portion folded under from the impact, and Dan lying beside it, not moving at all. I hustled down the slope to where he was. It was really bad. I carefully removed his helmet, which had a large indentation in the front of it. His face was turning blue, and I could see that he was not breathing. The truck driver shouted down to me that they had called 911 and the police and ambulance were on the way.

I started to give CPR to him at that time. Fortunately, I had gone through a class on CPR many years ago when in high school. The ambulance, actually an emergency rescue vehicle, came from Cleveland. I don't know how long it took for it to arrive. I had no sense of time while administering CPR. It has been estimated that I did CPR for almost 40 minutes until the paramedics arrived and immediately took over. Dan was loaded on to a stretcher and brought up the steep incline to the ambulance. I asked if I could travel with him to the hospital, and they complied.

That seemed to me as a terribly long trip. The ambulance driver was using flashing lights and siren, and still, many drivers on the road would not give way.

A little side note to all readers: when you see an emergency vehicle, make room for them to proceed. Someone's life could well depend on what you do.

The paramedic was doing everything she could, but still had to revive him several times on the way to the hospital. As we were entering the emergency drive, I heard one of them say, "we have to move fast. I think we may be losing him".

That is when the waiting began. Dan was in a coma for almost two weeks. The only thing the doctor would say is, "I don't know when or if he will come out of it, and I don't know what permanent damage has been done to his body or brain". This was obviously a very long week, sitting around the waiting room and hoping to get some positive news, and dreading the arrival of terrible news. Finally, the news came, and it was a combination of good and bad. He was out of the coma, and early signs indicate that his brain was functioning, but his spinal cord was severely damaged and he would never walk again. Knowing how hard this news was for me to accept, I could not fathom how it was going to hit Dan.

There were a lot of heroes that came into my life that day, Mary Ann and, Tyler, the paramedics who transported me to the hospital and kept me alive were among them. At an awards ceremony later that year, Mary Ann and Tyler would receive one of the most coveted awards a paramedic can be given, a Trauma Save, for their efforts that day. I found out later Mary Ann often came by the hospital and looked in on me to see how I was doing.

CHAPTER FOUR:
Trauma

"Without hope there is no need for any of us."
- Dan Miears

My wife Crissie's, day with no ending, in her own words:

Keep in mind, throughout this ordeal, there were NO cell phones!

That morning I was taking Dan over to John and Caren's because one of our cars was in the shop. They had planned a weekend of motorcycle riding. During the course of our conversation there, I found out that Wallace was John's middle name and I loved it. After dropping Dan off, I headed to work at Roberds in Norcross.

I meant to include an emergency contact list in Dan's wallet. At lunch, I realized I had forgotten to do that......the accident happened at lunch time. We went back to work from lunch to a normal crazy day in the world of retail when I received the call from John. All he told me was, "you need to get to the hospital" and I asked what was wrong. He said Dan is just unconscious. My friend, Bonny drove me to our townhouse. My parents were to pick me up from there and drive me to the hospital. I called my Dad and told him Dan had been in an accident and they needed to come get me. Dad left work and went to the grocery store to get Mom from shopping. While I waited on them to get there, I took the dog out, got a couple of insurance forms, and got clothes for Dan and me because I assumed he would be in the hospital overnight.

Dad and Mom picked me up and we made our long drive to Northeast Georgia Medical Center in Gainesville. When I got there, I entered through the emergency room. Everyone in that room bowed their heads when I came in. They took us to the prayer room where John was waiting. The doctor came in and said they thought Dan's aorta was ruptured and did I want to see him alive or did I want to wait because he was bleeding out. I said take me now. When I walked into the room, it was like the traumas you see on television. Dan was already posturing from the head injury, he was also swollen from the spinal shock and, they were bagging him. I asked the emergency room person bagging Dan what they were doing and he said, "I am breathing for him". I had never witnessed anything like it. I leaned over to Dan and told him he was tore up from head to toe and if he didn't fight like hell he would be gone within ten minutes. A tear ran down Dan's left cheek. He was completely unconscious and they were breathing for him, but I knew he heard me. We had recently had a conversation about life support and we both agreed we would want a chance to heal. I turned around to the hospital staff and said, "Do *whatever you have to do to keep him alive" and I walked out.*

I have not mentioned yet that I was five months pregnant. I did not get to see him again until around 9:00 that night. They took me to the admissions office and I remember having to sign so many documents. They asked me about life support machines and I asked them if he did not wake up after six weeks would we be able to take him off the machines. They said yes and I said hook him up to every machine you need to.

After I saw how bad Dan was, I called his Mom, Anne. She was working at her antique booth. I had just recently gotten her work phone number in case I went into labor and we needed to contact her. I told her he was seriously hurt and my Mom and Dad were on their way from Gainesville to pick her up.

The rest of the day and night is a blur. I remember being in the ICU waiting room. I remember all of the faces that were there with me, but I don't remember how they knew and when they got there. I do specifically remember when my sister arrived. Cyndi and Kenn were at the Baby Expo in Atlanta because she was also four months pregnant. There was no way to contact them. Kenn's parents taped a large sign across their garage door that Dan had been in an accident and they needed to get to Northeast Georgia Medical Center as soon as possible. So they immediately drove to Gainesville.

I did not get to see Dan until they had completed all kinds of tests. When I did get to go back, he was on a ventilator. We were told it would be an hour by hour wait to see if he would make it. He had a fractured neck, broken back, broken collar bone and scapula, broken ribs, broken hip socket, collapsed lung, and an anoxic head injury. Thankfully, they were wrong about the ruptured aorta. The anoxic head injury became their biggest concern.

Anoxic brain damage happens when the brain receives inadequate oxygen for several minutes or longer. Brain cells begin to die after approximately four minutes without oxygen. Dan had a Glasgow Coma Scale of 7 upon arrival at the emergency room. Emergency personnel typically determine the severity of a brain injury by using an assessment called the Glasgow Coma Scale (GCS). The terms Mild Brain Injury, Moderate Brain Injury, and Severe Brain Injury are used to describe the level of initial injury in relation to the neurological severity caused to the brain. A severe brain injury (GCS below 8) occurs when a prolonged unconscious state or coma lasts days, weeks, or months. (Source: Brain Injury Association of America)

As a precautionary measure, they had Dan in a medically induced coma to let his body rest and keep him from having seizures. I think this lasted about two weeks. I slept at his bedside and in the waiting room. We did not know once they took him off of the medication to keep him in a coma if he would wake up and if he woke up, what kind of shape he would be in. After the two weeks, they brought him out of the coma. He was confused and had lost about six weeks of memory. He did not remember our second wedding anniversary on August 15th. Every time he woke up, I would go through the story of what had happened. We had to restrain him because he kept pulling out the ventilator. He also managed to rip out the arterial line in his wrist. Dan did stabilize and was able to be moved out of ICU.

When Dan was moved to a regular room and the swelling had gone down, I discovered that something was very wrong. His upper jaw had detached from his skull. That put a whole new meaning to having a jacked up mouth. The first time they scheduled the surgery to reattach his jaw he came down with a staph infection and spiked a very high fever. He had to have ice blankets. The surgery had to be rescheduled. When they did the jaw surgery, he developed a blood clot in his lungs.

Our goal was to have Dan moved to the Shepherd Spinal Center. He failed his first evaluation. At that time, Shepherd was not a traumatic brain injury rehab facility and Dan was still confused and recovering from his head injury. One morning a few weeks after this happened, Dan woke up and asked what had happened, just like he had many times before. This time when I told him, he asked who had been paying our bills. I knew Dan was back! He said he had a life insurance policy and I said, "Well, you are still alive. You didn't even lose a toe, so we *can't even file a dismemberment claim." Dan's first reaction to what had happened was, "I am lucky to be alive" and, he has lived by that every moment of every day since!*

Dan was having a really rough day and I remember the nurse saying, "This is as good as it gets and the sooner you accept that the better you will be". How I did not get locked up that day is a miracle. I forcefully informed them that this WAS NOT as good as it gets. I had a recent issue of Shepherd Spinal Center's magazine, The Spinal Column, which had Bill Furbish on the cover in a swimming pool. I knew this was not as good as it gets.

Shepherd Spinal Center was created years earlier after James Shepherd had sustained a spinal cord injury himself. James Shepherd set out on a backpacking trip around the world in 1973 after graduating from the University of Georgia. While bodysurfing off a beach in Rio de Janeiro, he was slammed to the ocean floor by a wave. James, who was 22 at the time, sustained a serious spinal cord injury that left him paralyzed from the neck down.

After spending five weeks in a Brazilian hospital struggling to survive, he returned to the U.S. and with his parents - Alana and Harold Shepherd - located a rehabilitation treatment facility in Colorado. After six months of intensive rehabilitation, James regained his ability to walk while using a cane and a leg brace.

After returning home to Atlanta, the Shepherd family was frustrated with the lack of rehabilitation care options in the Southeast. With his parents' enthusiastic support, James founded Shepherd Center in 1975 as a six-bed unit operating out of leased space in an Atlanta hospital. Almost immediately there was a waiting list.

The Shepherds began recruiting support, first from old friends in the community, then from every individual, foundation, or corporation who might help back the facility. They also recruited David Apple, a young doctor who was willing to put long hours in to care for patients. Dr. Apple served as Medical Director from the beginning and now serves as Medical Director Emeritus.

In 1982, Shepherd Center moved to its current location on Peachtree Road in Atlanta's Buckhead neighborhood. The Center became a free-standing 80-bed facility. (Source: www.shepherd.org)

The Shepherd Center nurse came back and re-evaluated Dan and set the date for transfer. He received a halo before the transfer to stabilize his neck and back. Later at Shepherd Spinal Center, I thought it was difficult getting it on, but it was much worse having it taken off. Dan had no neck muscles at this point. When the nurse came in to take it off, I had to hold Dan's head to keep it from falling. The screws had become attached to his skin and it was tearing as they were pulling it off. It was one of the most difficult things I had to see Dan go through.

On moving day, as Dan lay on the stretcher, he had to give the ambulance drivers step by step directions to get from Gainesville to Shepherd. Once again, no cell phones, no GPS, no Map Quest.

I stayed at the hospital most of the time, but at some point I was able to go to my Aunt Burma and Uncle Hugh's house for a good night's sleep and much deserved shower. We had planned before the accident to move from our townhouse to a house in Lawrenceville. With the help of my family, I had to close up our townhouse and coordinate the move instead to John and Caren's house where Dan would join me after completing his rehabilitation.

I have been told by my family that I am one of the strongest, most courageous women ever. I know that the strength I have comes from the love and support of every single one of my family members.

CHAPTER FIVE:
A Journey Into Chaos: Brain and Spinal Cord Injury

"While the difficult takes time,
the impossible takes a little longer."
-Art Berg

On October 17, 1989, I was transferred to Shepherd Center in Atlanta, Georgia. On the way there, the paramedics transporting me were not sure of its location. Somehow, I gave them directions on how best to get there. I was not really sure what to expect upon my arrival but I hoped that it was one step closer to getting home, and, at the time, that's all that mattered.

Shepherd Center is the largest facility in the United States that specializes in treating and rehabilitating spinal cord injured persons. My head injury had improved to Rancho Los Amigos Scale 6, which was necessary for my acceptance into their rehab program.

The Rancho Los Amigos Levels of Cognitive Functioning is an evaluation tool used by the rehabilitation team. The eight levels describe the patterns or stages of recovery typically seen after a brain injury. This helps the team understand and focus on the person's abilities and design an appropriate treatment program. Each person will progress at their own rate, depending on the severity of the brain damage, the location of the injury in the brain, and the length of time since the brain injury. Some individuals will pass through each of the eight levels, while others may progress to a certain level and fail to change to the next higher level.

A Rancho Scale of 6 meant I was at an appropriate level to begin rehabilitation.

COGNITIVE LEVEL VI
CONFUSED AND APPROPRIATE
A person at this level may:
• be somewhat confused because of memory and thinking problems. He will remember the main points from a conversation, but forget and confuse the details. For example, he may remember he had visitors in the morning, but forget what they talked about;
• follow a schedule with some assistance, but becomes confused by changes in the routine;
• know the month and year, unless there is a severe memory problem;
• pay attention for about 30 minutes, but has trouble concentrating when it is noisy or when the activity involves many steps.

(Source: the Rancho Los Amigos Family Guide to Cognitive Functioning)

My short-term memory was most affected by the head injury. I would find out later that, with an anoxic head injury, timing is critical in starting CPR. If CPR is administered in the first 3 to 5 minutes there is a chance of having no significant or permanent damage.

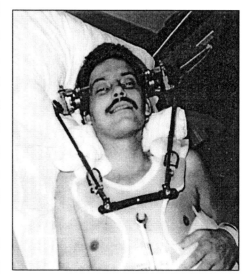

We have estimated that my dad started CPR within two to three minutes of my injury and that made all the difference. If he had started CPR much later than that, my anoxic head injury could have been very severe with very little chance of any recovery. I could not recall the several days before my injury with much clarity, but days prior to that, I seemed to be able to recall with greater accuracy.

Because of the head injury, I was also diagnosed with Post-Concussion Syndrome.

Traumatic Brain Injury (TBI) impairs the ability to think, do, and know. Memory, mood and attention are the top three complaints of brain injury patients. Intellectual dullness and mental rigidity are apparent signs of brain injury. Personality changes are common, and rapid mood swings alternate with waxing and waning energy levels. The overall effect can be profoundly disabling. (Source: Brain injury Resource Center)

I still had my Halo on and my mouth was still wired shut with arch bars and I looked terrible. Evidently, it appears, sometime in the night the "Snap-On-Tools" Fairy came to visit me and gave me a crescent wrench. I would find out later that I was placed on the Halo vest in the event that I went into cardiac arrest. They would then be able to detach the Halo from the vest and administer CPR.

Later, I would learn that everyone arriving at Shepherd Spinal Center is taken to x-ray on the first floor and the journey on the tile floor made for a bumpy ride. Upon getting into the x-ray room, the gurney was not in far enough and the door closed and hit my Halo. Nothing serious, but the jolt surprised me and I thought, "Wow, this is going to be a fun place". After the x-ray experience, I was taken to the intensive care unit. Shepherd Center is truly a unique place and was the only freestanding rehabilitation facility that had its own intensive care unit. That's still true today.

As I discovered later, Shepherd Center was the best place I could've gone. As much as I needed rehabilitation, the first attention was given to the medical complications that followed my initial injury. In the five weeks since I'd been injured, I had lost a significant amount of weight, from 215 pounds to 155 pounds. My nutritional stores were wiped out and I had a Stage IV pressure ulcer that was getting worse by the day.

> **Pressure ulcers**, also known as **decubitus ulcers** or **bedsores**, are localized injuries to the skin and/or underlying tissue usually over a <u>bony</u> prominence, as a result of pressure, or pressure in combination with shear and/or friction. Most commonly this will be the sacrum, coccyx, heels or the hips, but other sites such as the elbows, knees, ankles or the back of the cranium can be affected.

> **Stage IV**: Full thickness tissue loss with exposed bone, tendon or muscle. Slough or eschar may be present on some parts of the wound bed. Often include undermining and tunneling. The depth of a stage IV pressure ulcer varies by anatomical location. Exposed bone/tendon is visible or directly palpable. In 2012, the NPUAP stated that pressure ulcers with exposed cartilage are also classified as a stage IV. (Source: Medline Plus)

I was introduced to the team that was going to be responsible for my recovery and rehabilitation. Cheryl Linden was my occupational therapist, as true a smart class clown of a person as you could ever want to meet. She made the difficult and mundane tasks entertaining and mostly enjoyable. Debbie Backus, my physical therapist, always had this offbeat sense of humor that would throw me off whatever task I was working on at the time. My primary nurse, Carol Stevens, had a calm sense about her that never made me get too freaked out when something wouldn't go quite right.

Leslie Smith was the social worker who would be working on my discharge plan home, whenever that was going to be. And then there was Dr. Apple, who was the physician assigned to my care and, as I found out later, was also the Medical Director of Shepherd Center.

There was a whole support cast of night and weekend nurses and other therapists and healthcare professionals who would pitch in if they felt that you were slacking off in the least bit.   Jill Koval, one of the psychologists at Shepherd Center, would be working with my wife and me to work through the emotional recovery from my injury.   There was also Steve Sloan, a psychologist/sex guru who explained that things would be different now with a complete spinal cord injury. With no sensation or feeling below my level of injury, sex now had a new definition and rulebook.

CHAPTER SIX:
The Tortoise And The Hare

*"No matter how many times you read it,
the tortoise always wins."*
- Alex G Spanos

Alex G. Spanos is the owner of the San Diego Chargers and A G Spanos' Construction. During an interview by a reporter from the New York Times, he was asked what his favorite book was. He replied, 'The Tortoise and the Hare. No matter how many times you read it, the tortoise always wins." Life for us is not a race to the top; it's a race unique and different for each of us. This race to the finish line is the culmination of many small steps that slowly build over time and you pick up momentum to get to there. For me, this race of recovery would be slow, with numerous setbacks and I could not measure my recovery to that of other patients. I was on my own tortoise pace.

As time went on, I was moved to Room (Cell) 203, a four bed ward and was assigned to bed C, which I would occupy for most of the six months during my rehabilitation. I didn't realize it at the time, but my wife must have signed a six-month lease for Room 203 bed C.

For almost the next two months, I would live in the bed that was allocated to that part of the room and perform all of life's daily functions there. Bed baths, bowel programs, intermittent catheterizations, all meals, and sleep (when I could get it). With three other roommates in the same room, there was always a constant buzz of noise and activity around. If it wasn't the intercom system sounding off trying to locate a nurse, it was a roommate snoring or one of us, periodically, receiving attention from the medical staff that made sound sleep an almost impossible task.

I tried some disposable ear plugs to deaden the noise. This helped and I was able to start tuning out all of the nighttime activity that filled the room.

During my time there, almost all of my roommates were injured falling out of a deer stand. Two of my roommates were hunting together and both fell out of their deer stands 100 yards from each other. So I asked them which one of them went for help, ha ha. After being in a place for 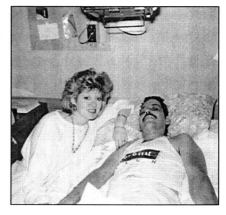 so long, you can't help but start to find humor in almost everything.

One of the night nurses had a special caring way about her and would kiss me on the forehead and tell me good night. With her tucking me in at night, there was a sense of peace to the chaos of the day and, at that moment, a little bit of normalcy returned. It was like a flashback to my childhood with mom tucking me in at night when I was little, telling me that everything was OK, and that there was no boogie man under the bed waiting to pounce on me when the lights went out. Although battered by my injuries, I wasn't totally consumed by devastation; and would live to fight another day!

I wish I could recall that nurse's name. After about a month or so of being my night nurse, she and her husband decided to take traveling nurse positions in Hawaii. I'm not sure where they went after that.

If you ever read this book, I want you to know that you made falling asleep a little easier and the endless interruptions of nurses checking up on me and my roommates more tolerable. Thank you!

All of the nurses had their own special way of showing they really cared about you and in the care they provided. Some had their own quirkiness about them that added to the interactions with them. Thank you to all of the nurses and therapists who were part of the care I received while at Shepherd, you are all truly angels.

Due to my medical conditions, I was not able to sit up in a wheelchair, so I would travel around the hospital in my bed. Initially, I would not spend much time outside my room. While therapies were going on in the gym, I would be spending my time watching all the wonderful reruns on the TBS channel in my room. When possible, my bed and I would attend therapies in the gym, the educational key classes, and other functions the same as other patients. It surely was medical incarceration at its worst. Although my team tried to make sure I attended everything the other patients did, my bed stuck out like a broken bus. My nickname, I believe, became "The Bed Guy".

CHAPTER SEVEN:
History

*"None of us can change what has happened,
but we can change what happens next."*
- Dan Miears

You don't have to be at Shepherd Center for too long to realize that something crummy has happened to everyone that comes there. No one set out on the morning they got injured saying, "Wow, I think I want to go break my neck or back or get a head injury today". As you think you may have it bad, there is always someone else there that's in worse shape than you are. There are also others whose injuries were not as severe as yours. Needless to say, it's hard to have a pity party and feel like no one else knows what you're going through.

For a majority of the life-changing events that occur in people's lives, there is little fanfare, no articles in the newspaper and, other than the network of your friends, family and coworkers, most people will never know you or your story. Now, with the Internet and social media, the tragic news can travel around the world with just a couple of clicks of the mouse.

Ultimately, I had to make a decision, was I going to be remembered for my accident, or was I going to be remembered for how I responded to it. You have to decide if you're going to live your life as a victim and forever use how you got hurt as an excuse for not moving forward in life. Some people's injuries were caused by someone else or something else they had no control of.

If you live your life as a History Major and can't move past a tragic event, you will never move forward. Some will forever blame others for their "lot in life" and will forever be a victim of the events in their life.

"You can blame someone for an event in your life,
you can't blame them for the rest of your life."
- Author Unknown

Sometimes, things just happen in our lives that are out of our control. Curly, of the Three Stooges, often remarked, "I'm a victim of circumstance". Stuff happens.

It's often been said that, "Life is 10% of what occurs in your life and 90% of how you react or respond to it". It's no more complicated than that. You have to make the decision. Are you going to focus on the 10% that you cannot change, or the 90% you have complete control over? The choice is yours to make as to which one you choose to focus your efforts and energy on.

"It's not whether you get knocked down,
it's whether you get back up."
- Vince Lombardi

For Halloween, the always comical Cheryl Linden decided that "the bed guy" should be a deck of playing cards. So the next thing I knew, I had playing cards taped all around my Halo, all around my bed, and a big playing card on my chest. I don't recall there being

a Halloween costume contest but as best she could, I was dressed for Halloween. I think maybe a better costume for me would've been a "bedbug".

When I would go to the gym (prison yard) in my bed, I was limited to what therapies I could do. I had atrophied so much on my right side that, in order to shake someone's hand, I would have to pick up my right hand with my left hand and extend it out to shake. I once was handed a 4 ounce barbell to start working out with. It looked like a toy and probably was.

One of the team events in the gym was beach ball volleyball. They would put me on the back row to participate in the game, but, actually, I believe that I was a target and I'm not sure that even the quadriplegics wanted me on their team. I had one good arm I could flail around in the air and try and hit the ball as it ever so slowly would come my way.

I recall one time in the yard watching the other patients work out. I noticed one of the other patients, David Coffee putting on leg braces. Shortly thereafter, a dashing young doctor named Dr. Leslie came in to observe and work with him and his therapist. I realized that I obviously wasn't a candidate for that program. David was a very hard worker and likable guy and determined to literally get back on his feet.

The Human Resources Director for Shepherd Spinal Center, later approached David about coming to work in her department to assist employees with their retirement plans and benefits. He turned her down and wanted to get back to St. Louis and the life he had left there. I realized that as much as I wanted to find work, I didn't qualify for that job either. I was jealous of the opportunity David had and realized I would have a lot of work ahead to make the most of my situation.

Thanksgiving rolled around and I finally started to regain my appetite. Thanksgiving dinner was brought to my room and there were plates and plates of food. My wife was approaching eight months of pregnancy and had never lost her appetite. She helped me consume most of the meal. I'm not sure how she kept up with everything going on. All of the stress of having to deal with my injury, being pregnant and going back to work would be too much for most to take. What an incredible woman! I am still in awe of her to this day.

Finally, a flap surgery was scheduled to repair my sacral wound and Dr. Apple performed the surgery. Flap surgery is a technique in plastic and reconstructive surgery where any type of tissue is lifted from a donor site and moved to a recipient site with an intact blood supply.

Years later, in a conversation with Dr. Apple over lunch, I complemented him on his great work and asked, as an orthopedic surgeon, how he developed the skills to do such a masterful flap surgery. He said that he had done an internship on hand surgery. I'm not sure how that qualified him to work on my rear end but he did an incredible job. Twenty three years later, it's still holding up.

As any artist would do, he carved his initials DA to the left of his master piece! Just kidding, but one of the nurses remarked that, as usual, Dr. Apple always signed his great works of art.

Back in the Prison Yard (the gym), you could not take a break and relax if your guard (therapist) was called away, the other guards would always keep a watchful eye on you and notice the slightest bit of slacking off. Guards like Linda Maynard who, pound for pound, could take on anyone, or Sarah Morrison, another young gun physical therapist, would get tremendous glee in getting on to you.

Karla was the physical therapy assistant that I loved to hate the most. She was stern but caring. After I had my halo removed, she would always snatch the extra pillows out from under my head when I came into the yard. She said, "You don't want to have your chin resting on your chest the rest of your life, do you?" As uncomfortable as that made me, she really cared about me and didn't want me to have a crooked neck the rest of my life. She always expected nothing but your best effort, anything less and she was going to call you out on it!

Seriously though, all of the guards (therapists) would give you the tough love of a virtual hug and a noogie to push you to your full potential. I am thankful for all of the attention they gave me in the yard and on trash detail outside the compound. Just kidding about the trash detail, but I'm sure they probably thought about it.

I have never been in prison, but joke about the similarity of a rehabilitation hospital and a prison. In both places, you're in a different and somewhat restricted environment, far removed from your life back home. You have visitors and prior tenants offering peer support. You hear about life outside but it seems to be so far away. You have essentially, temporarily, checked out of your life and are focused on recovering. There are a lot of supportive services to rehabilitate you and concentrate on maximizing your quality of life and independence upon your return home. Neither place wants to see you back except as a visitor.

CHAPTER EIGHT:
Freedom

"He who has truly overcome his fears will truly be free."
– Aristotle

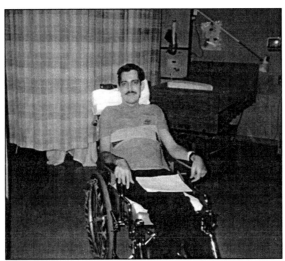

Freedom Day, December 15, 1989

Dan Miears is released from medical incarceration, Room 203 Bed C. I finally have four wheels under my atrophied rear end and can go anywhere I want, well almost, at least as far as 15 minutes of freedom would get me. The first wheelchair they put me in was a beauty, 80 pounds of chrome and plastic. It was a behemoth of a manual chair. It had a reclining back and leg rests that would be raised up and put into action every 30 minutes for weight shift. Parole began and those 15 minutes was all the time that I was allowed to be up in a chair before I had to get back in bed and have the nurse or therapist check my skin to make sure everything was okay. I needed to continue to exhibit good behavior and keep up with my kitchen timer that every thirty minutes signified it was time for weight shift. Over time, my sitting tolerance would be increased with the long-term goal of getting to the point I could stay up in a wheelchair all day.

During my medical incarceration, Pat Driscoll, who worked in the Therapeutic Recreation Department, used to come by and ask me all the time what I liked to do. I kept saying I don't know. One-time she asked if I was interested in wood carving. I said, "Sure", so she handed me a block of wood with the beginnings of a Santa Claus face and body partially carved out, an X-Acto knife and a book about carving antique looking Santa Clauses. I was still on Coumadin, a blood thinner I had to take due to a clot I had in my leg. What could go wrong? Well, fortunately, nothing went wrong. At night, I would hack away on the block of wood to give it some resemblance to one of the Santas in the book. I'm sure housekeeping hated it, because as the wood shavings would accumulate on top of my bed, I would just fluff my sheets and would send them off to the floor without a care in the world. My goal was to carve one or two Santas to give as Christmas gifts.

Now that I was actively participating in therapy, the next goal was to be able to go home for Christmas on a weekend pass. I worked very hard to try and improve, but it was slow going. My team ultimately decided to approve my going home for the weekend. Home, however, was not the home that I left the morning of my accident. The townhome that my wife and I lived in was no longer an option and the house that we were going to be moving into was also long gone. My wife, with the help of our friends and families, moved our belongings out and placed them in storage in several family members' homes.

Home now, at least initially, was going to be living with my dad and stepmom. We were to occupy the downstairs guest bedroom. But it still was someplace that we could go and be alone with each other. This was going to be an awkward experience, for my wife and I had not slept in the same bed since before my injury. Trying to retain any sense of a relationship during all of this was difficult at best.

December 22, 1989, time to go home for the holidays. With some reluctance, my rehab team decided to let me go home for Christmas to be with my family. My sitting tolerance at that time was a robust 45 minutes. So me, my behemoth wheelchair with all of its attachments, a Hoyer lift, too many medical supplies to mention, and a lot of anxiety loaded up to move into my dad's downstairs guestroom for the weekend. As much as I enjoyed being out of the big house and being around my family, it was an arduous task for my family to tend to my needs. I was still very dependent on others and felt bad about needing their assistance with the simplest of things. But, we were together and Christmas that year had a special meaning because I had begun to realize that life is a very fragile thing, that we take way too much for granted, and don't appreciate the things both big and small that we have.

I had completed the task of carving my Santa Claus with all my fingers still intact and felt that I had created something, which for me, was a lasting statement. That primitive looking Santa Claus was a major accomplishment, for I had created something out of nothing and gave it to someone as a gift.

Overall, the weekend went without a hitch. We only had to call the second floor nurses' station several times to discuss possible medical issues we thought I was having. I'm sure that everyone was relieved when I checked back in to Room 203 Bed C.

We took our experience from our first weekend pass and applied it to the following weekend pass, New Year's Eve weekend. Friday evening, I and all my medical stuff went back to my dad's house and settled in that afternoon. Saturday morning my wife woke up at 4 AM, her water broke, and she went into labor. Well, that certainly was a big surprise for us; because my son's expected due date was not for another week or two. So she and my stepmom, Caren, rushed off to the hospital.

My dad and I were left to try and get me and my 80-pound Cadillac wheelchair to the hospital. By the time we arrived, Crissie had already checked in and started a difficult labor that would finally end with a Cesarean section at 10:13 that Sunday morning.

CHAPTER NINE:
Why Am I Still Here?

"The Purpose of life is a life of purpose."
– Robert Byrne

December 31, 1989, one of the greatest events in my life occurred. That morning, our son was born. I was in the operating room when he came into this world and I was given one of the answers to one of the questions that I had struggled to answer since 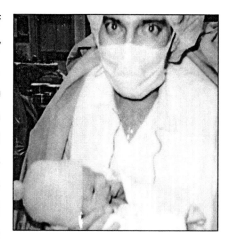 my injury. Having survived a horrific event, there must be some great deed that I still needed to accomplish with my life. As I held my son in my hands, I thought, maybe being there for him and being the best Dad that he could ever have, might be enough! Certainly that would be worthy of a deed given to any man.

The role of parents and their importance in a child's life, I think, is lost in today's society. The value of a child having two parents in their life cannot be overstated. I know there are many single parents out there that are doing a great job raising their children. When possible, it's best to have both parents in their child's life. I just know for me how important my adopted dad, John, has been in my life and I was thankful for the opportunity to be in my son's life.

The hospital was very gracious and they actually put my wife and me into a semi-private room, giving her one bed and me the other. Both beds were pushed together and we passed our son back and forth to each other and to the grandparents and family members. It was truly quite a celebration. The weekend pass ended and I returned once again to Shepherd Center.

I was more motivated when I returned to continue and finish my rehabilitation but was still concerned about what I was going to do to get a job.

My greatest loss after the physical ones was my job. I loved what I did and the people that I worked with. All I wanted to do was to go back to work and, if I could've done just that, then all of the woes of being paralyzed would seem less significant. The job you have is important; it gives you membership into society. In any conversation with a stranger, the question is always ultimately asked, "so what kind of work do you do?" I had always worked hard and provided an income for myself and going back to an outside sales position, calling on homeowners, was not going to be in my future.

I started working with Eileen DeWayne, a vocational counselor with the state of Georgia. Eileen, who was a paraplegic herself, understood the challenges that I would face and was very supportive in my talks with her. I took a vocational evaluation to determine what I might be good at and provide some direction to my future. Upon conclusion of the test and its results, I was given the opportunity to go back to school with vocational services paying for my classes and books.

It was thought that I should consider Georgia Tech and get a degree in Industrial Design or I could go to Georgia State and pursue a business degree. I had never really liked school before, but I understood that, if I was going to have the greatest opportunity to find gainful employment, I would need an education that would once again make me a worthy candidate for any job that I wished to pursue.

Crissie, working with our social worker Leslie, had filed for Social Security Disability Insurance (SSDI) and was told that I would start receiving SSDI payments six months after the date of my injury. It was a painful thing to accept, that I would now be dependent on this check to show up in the mail on the third of each month. It would not replace the income I had before my injury but it was better than nothing. That and the help of our families made it possible for me to move forward on going back to school.

"If you think an education is expensive,
you should try ignorance."
- A Harvard Professor

Education can come in many forms, through life experiences and formal education in the classroom.

Knowledge itself, though, is meaningless if you don't apply it in your daily life. I have often told my children, "It's not what you know but what you show." You can be the smartest person on the planet but if you show ignorance by not using that knowledge then you are no better off for knowing it.

I was probably the butter knife in the drawer before my accident. The accident itself broke my blade, though; and I now had a new edge, a sharper, keener edge that allowed me to refocus my efforts on what was important for me and my family.

At 31 years of age, I was going back to school; woo hoo, what a rush! I had never truly excelled in any subject; I always struggled with English, grammar, and math. I was still angry for this change in my life, but was determined to give it everything I could in pursuit of gaining my financial freedom once again with employment. I didn't know where I would eventually find work. I just hoped this would lead to something worthwhile.

For me, I was going to have to find a new way to fish! We have all heard the saying, "Give a man a fish and you feed him for a day, show him how to fish and you feed him for a lifetime." For me it was quite simple, I could sit around and wait for that fish (Social Security check) to show up the third of each month the rest of my life and be dependent on that fish to show up each month, or I could go out and learn how to fish again, become self-reliant, and regain my financial independence. That was my goal.

CHAPTER TEN:

Let's Go Camping and Feed the Lions and Tigers

"It takes a lot of courage to release the familiar and seemingly secure, to embrace the new. But there is no real security in what is no longer meaningful. There is more security in the adventurous and exciting, for in movement there is life and in change there is power."
- Alan Cohen

One of the therapeutic recreational specialists said, "Let's go camping", as they entered my room. I thought how can this be possible? I'm still living in a hospital. These camping trips were something that Shepherd Center was known for. Once a month they would get together a group of inpatients and go off camping for the weekend. I was told that we would be going out to Red Palmer's place. Red was the man who perfected use of the tranquilizer dart that is now used throughout the world to sedate animals, big and small. Although retired, he still had his compound located near Douglasville, Georgia.

We would have the opportunity to go fishing and see some of the wildlife that he still had at his compound. So we loaded up that Friday afternoon and headed out into the wilderness.

Red Palmer was a very interesting man. He had traveled the world and had artifacts of his travels throughout his office. He said that often Marlon Perkins, who had a popular TV show, "Mutual of Omaha's Wild Kingdom", used to often follow him around and do his shows in the same area where Red was.

Although retired, he still kept some exotic animals at his compound. He had hyenas and elk to name a few, but I was most intrigued that he raised lions and tigers in captivity. In fact, they were kept behind a normal 5 foot tall chain link fence in front of his house. So, as I was rolling around the compound that weekend the phrase, "Meals on Wheels"

took on a whole new meaning. You don't have to watch too many National Geographic specials to know the slowest animal in the herd is often the first one eaten. So as I was pushing around in my wheelchair that weekend, I made sure I wasn't last in the food line and was out pushing the power wheelchairs. I don't believe that I have ever slowed down.

CHAPTER ELEVEN:
Life Past The Parking Lot. What Next?

"Don't stunt your own growth worrying about what other people have that you don't."
- Neal Boortz

March 16, 1990 Graduation Day at Shepherd Center

The day had come! Six and a half months after my accident, it was time to go home and not come back. This was a day of mixed emotions of what would happen next. Shepherd Center had been my home, a place of security and comfort, and it would be hard to leave all that behind. By this time, some members of my initial rehabilitation team had been replaced. Maybe I just wore them out. But this was a great group of dedicated specialists that made it their life's work to help people get back to life and get to higher ground.

I had many Sherpas along the way, my dad for his heroic efforts in keeping me alive, Mary Ann and Tyler for getting me to Northeast Georgia Medical Center, all of the doctors, nurses, and therapists as well as countless other strangers who all came into my life in my time of need. I had the right people, at the right place, at the right time and none of them gave up, even though a positive outcome looked doubtful.

I was going to make sure that all of their effort and energy expended to help me would not go waste. I owed it to them, all of them, to make something of myself and become someone that they could be proud of.

That weekend Crissie and I wanted to get away, so we drove up to Helen, Georgia to spend a couple of nights away from everyone and have some time to ourselves. On the way to Helen, we stopped to see Mary Ann in Cleveland. I wanted to thank her for all of her efforts on the fateful day of my accident. Had I not gotten hurt, we would've never crossed paths, but, because we did, I will be forever grateful for her saving my life. Before we left, she gave me a framed Ziggy needlepoint she had done that featured Ziggy holding a flower and said "love is good for growing things". Thank

God for people like Mary Ann and Tyler, who unselfishly give of themselves on a daily basis to come to the aid of complete strangers in their time of crises.

Now came the hard part. I had to stay on top of my health and make good decisions regarding how I lived each day. I had to work on renewing my relationship with

my wife and I knew that I needed to be someone that she would want to be with. For my son, I had to continue to learn how to be a father and the best parent I could for him from a wheelchair. I had to 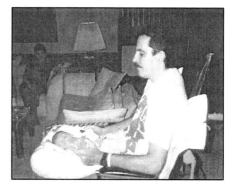 work on trying to fit in again into the world that I had left seven months ago and understand that it would not be the same as before.

I looked into volunteering opportunities at Shepherd Center and other places in the community. Finally, the ultimate challenge was to go to school, get a degree in something, find meaningful work, and become independent once again.

CHAPTER TWELVE:
Fish Notice Water Last

"It's been said that fish notice water last."
-French Proverb

Fish live their whole life submerged in a beautiful and liquid world full of color and beauty. Water, the most important element of their survival, is right before their eyes and they aren't even aware of its importance in their lives.

Are you aware of what's most important in your life? If you are in reasonably good health, there are many people that are not. If you have enough to eat, there are some who will go to bed hungry tonight. If you have children, even rebellious ones, there are some who would give anything to have even one child of their own. If you're fortunate to still have one or both of your parents still living, there are some who would give anything to be able to pick up the phone right now and call their mom or dad and say," Hey, how are you doing, I love you". It's all in what you notice first and what's important in life. What are the most important things in your life? What are those most precious things and people in your life that you notice last until they are gone? What is your water?

CHAPTER THIRTEEN:
Pursuit of Freedom

"If one advances confidently in the direction of one's dreams, and endeavors to live the life which one has imagined, one will meet with a success unexpected in common hours."
- Henry David Thoreau

The "pursuit of freedom", isn't that really what we all want; to be in charge of our own lives and control our own destiny? Not to rely on someone else to decide for us? The pursuit of freedom, of independence, is withering away before our very eyes. As a society, we are becoming more and more dependent on others and the government to decide and provide for us. As you take something, you give something up in return - your freedom, until you become totally dependent on someone else. That's a terrible way to go through life. I know for some their injuries or ailments are so severe and needs are so great that they need a lifetime of assistance and support just to get through each day. That assistance and support often isn't enough and the majority of care falls onto the loved ones. I do believe that every person has something meaningful to add and contribute.

There are many people who have all of their physical capability, but do not have any desire to do anything meaningful. Their paralysis comes from accepting the payoffs of government subsidies in return for not trying to better themselves. My hope is that, regardless of someone's condition or situation, they can find a way to be a contributing member to our society and add their unique gifts to the fabric of our lives.

One of the best examples of someone with the greatest of limitations harboring one of the greatest gifts of mankind is Stephen W. Hawking.

"All of my life, I have been fascinated by the big questions that face us, and have tried to find scientific answers to them. If, like me, you have looked at the stars, and tried to make sense of what you see, you too have started to wonder what makes the universe exist."
- Stephen W. Hawking

In 1963, Hawking contracted motor neuron disease and was given two years to live. Yet he went on to Cambridge to become a brilliant researcher and Professorial Fellow at Gonville and Caius College. Since 1979 he has held the post of Lucasian Professor at Cambridge, the chair held by Isaac Newton in 1663. Professor Hawking has over a dozen honorary degrees and was awarded the CBE in 1982. He is a fellow of the Royal Society and a Member of the US National Academy of Science. Stephen Hawking is regarded as one of the most brilliant theoretical physicists since Einstein.

In spite of being wheelchair bound and dependent on a computerized voice system for

communication Stephen Hawking continues to combine family life (he has three children and three grandchildren), and his research into theoretical physics together with an extensive program of travel and public lectures. He still hopes to make it into space one day.
(Source: http://www.hawking.org.uk)

Stephen proves that life is not limited by our deficiencies, but by our imagination and determination to pursue that which is in our own human spirit.

CHAPTER FOURTEEN:
Motivation

"Motivation is like bathing, we recommend it daily."
- Zig Zeigler

You are, ultimately, a product of your environment. You become what and who surrounds you. I realized a long time ago that for me to stay positive and upbeat, I would have to surround myself with people who were always positive and upbeat. I knew that for me to keep that attitude with the challenges I would confront, I would need to find these people after my injury. I looked for successful persons with spinal cord injury in or around Shepherd Center. Some were Shepherd Center employees; Bill Furbish, Mark Johnson, and Bert Burns.

Bill Furbish was a very accomplished athlete who had won numerous awards and worked in the IT department at Shepherd Center.

Mark Johnson was the Disability Advocate at Shepherd Center and had been part of several disability organizations that fought for the rights and freedom of persons with disabilities. Mark had been arrested more than once during disability movement events.

Bert Burns had been one of the therapeutic recreation specialists that I had worked with while at Shepherd Center. Bert was an accomplished athlete as well and would later leave Shepherd Center to go start a very successful company called Uromed.

As I got to know and become friends with them and other former patients of Shepherd Center, I would try and learn from them about their successes and failures in obtaining a meaningful life and employment. There were a lot of other great people that I would meet who, although not seeking employment, had found a meaningful life in other pursuits. I want to be clear here, employment is not the only measure of a person, but for me it was one that had high priority.

As you go through life, there are many people who will cross your path, some can offer wisdom and others can only offer despair. I have always tried to learn from each and, when possible, offer words of encouragement and wisdom to those who feel that their life has no purpose or direction. We all get lost in life from time to time and need someone to help us get back on track. Having said that, there are some people who are more than content with their misery and feel obligated to give some of that misery to you. Life is hard, and you're never truly beyond recovery unless you give up. Never give up!

CHAPTER FIFTEEN:
With Change Comes Opportunity

"It is never too late to be who you might have been."
- George Eliot

If you sit still and do nothing, you will change nothing in your life, and if change does come your way, it will probably not be to your liking. Some people will live their entire lives waiting for something good to happen, waiting for luck and good fortune to find them. MOVE! Do something every day to improve your life. The greatest success in life is the completion of many small things focused on accomplishing one great thing.

For me, I had to make a decision. Did I want to be remembered for my accident, and all the empathy, pity, and sorrow that came with it? Or, did I want to be remembered for how I reacted or responded to my injury? I chose the latter of the two. With every change in your life, there comes a new opportunity and a new direction. Volunteering, ultimately, allowed me to travel in different circles and meet new people that I might never have crossed paths with. Volunteering, I believe, is a gateway activity that can lead to many new opportunities. It can build and build to more opportunities, which could lead to being valued and needed once again.

I started volunteering. I began as a peer supporter at Shepherd Center and volunteered for their Speakers Bureau. The Americans with Disabilities Act had recently passed, and there was an opportunity to go out and speak with various businesses about what it meant, and the proper etiquette when interacting with people with disabilities.

It was at this time that I had the opportunity to participate in an advertising campaign promoting the hiring of persons with disabilities. I was pictured in an ad that ran in various

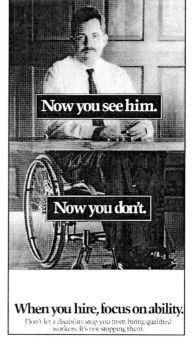

business journals. The picture was quite compelling and speaks for itself. With my new appearance, I have developed a tremendous sense of understanding and appreciation of the challenges that women and minorities have faced being sized up just by your physical appearance. My wheelchair may be the most obvious thing about me, but is the least of who I am as a person. I'm 6'5" tall, but now, depending on what convenience store I leave, I am 4'6" tall to 4'8" tall. To quote Larry the Cable Guy, "that's funny, I don't care who you are".

"My wheelchair may be the first thing people notice,
but it's the least of who I am as a person."
– Robert Antonisse

For me, my hope is the wheelchair is the last thing people remember, and that's up to me. Whatever it is the people notice about you first, is probably the least of who you are as a person. We're often placed in groups related to these most obvious features; our skin color, our size, our shape, our disability. Until you project yourself past what's obvious about you as an individual, all anyone will ever see you as is a member of whatever group you represent. Celebrate your uniqueness as an individual and breakaway from whatever the group stereotypes you're associated with.

CHAPTER SIXTEEN:
No Place Like Home

*"There is no place more delightful
than one's own fireplace."*
- Marcus Tulius Cicero

After living with my parents for several months, it was quite clear that we needed more room. So we started the impossible task of finding an affordable, wheelchair accessible apartment in Atlanta. We finally found an accessible apartment that was reasonable on the corner of Jimmy Carter Blvd. and Buford Highway. What a scary, crazy place that turned out to be. The apartment was very accessible, but it was an old apartment building that had numerous problems and was not in a very safe area.

After months of dealing with cockroaches that would not go away, we were able to break our lease and move into a new apartment complex on Boggs Road. I continued to go to Georgia State and volunteer at Shepherd Center, as time allowed. As the months passed, the new apartment complex was getting worse with crime and we knew we would have to, once again, start looking for another place to live.

By that time, my son and I had become quite a pair. We would go shopping by ourselves and do other things, and my wife would always worry about our safe return. We were very close and I believe he always saw just me. The chair was just something for him to climb on or push around. He loved to sit in my lap or on my feet and that was one of his favorite places to hang out.

I heard about this loan for first time homeowners, it had an income qualifying component to it and had a maximum loan amount of $82,000. So, the hunt was on. Where do you find a house for $82,000? After looking around for several months you find an $82,000 house in Winder, Georgia, where I jokingly say, "Winder is where front porches are considered bonus rooms". Actually, it's a great place to live and still has a great sense of community. I found this builder who was building all brick homes for $80,000. Jerry Peck, a prince of a guy from Watkinsville, Georgia, said he would build us a house. And did he build us a house! We ended up with an all brick constructed home with a 2½ car garage big enough for my minivan with the lift and raised roof.

October 1992, we moved into our new home with an unbelievable house warming surprise. My wife said, "Dan, we are going to have another child"! I couldn't believe what I heard. Steve Sloan, the Sex Psychologist at Shepherd Center told us during our counseling sessions that we didn't need to worry about birth control. As a complete spinal cord injured male, the only way we could have another child would be with medical assistance and use of a fertility clinic. The chances were, **"One in 1 Million"**, LIAR!!!!

While in school at Georgia State I would often visit the library and look up articles and publications regarding issues with spinal cord injury. I found one story a quadriplegic had written regarding intimacy with his girlfriend. It was very informative, and in it he explained how he was still able to have an orgasm in spite of being a complete spinal cord injury with no sensation below his level of injury. We tried his technique and it worked. We still didn't think we would be able to have another child on our own, but where there is a will, there is a way. We didn't see that one coming, but felt fortunate that we were blessed to be having another child.

Take that Dr. Sloan! HA! We will be laughing all the way to the Maternity Ward.

John and I doing one of our wheelies in the house, much to the dismay of my wife who always thought we were going to fall out. We never did!

CHAPTER SEVENTEEN:
A Quantum Leap of Faith

"All of the world is made of faith, trust and Pixie Dust."
- J M Barrie, Peter Pan

All of those months volunteering at Shepherd Center paid off. I was offered a part-time job funded by the Medicaid Indigent Care Trust Fund. The fund is a reimbursement fund that Shepherd Center receives from the federal government as partial reimbursement for treating Medicaid recipients. The job itself entailed working with a nurse and educating the medical community on care and treatment of spinal cord injured persons. They had hired a wonderful nurse to work with me, Pat Hancock. The position itself was 30 hours a week and paid $12 an hour. It wasn't much, but it was a start.

It was the beginning I was hoping for in my pursuit of being employed full-time once again. There was no real job description, as they left it up to us to figure out how to best provide education and resources to medical professionals in Georgia. I was still carrying a full class load at Georgia State at the time. The official start date was to be January 12, 1993. When I registered for the following winter semester, I selected mostly night classes so as not to interfere with my day job.

There was no guarantee that the position was a permanent one since it hinged on federal funding. Also, this started my trial work period with Social Security. At that time, you had a nine-month trial work period and past that, if you continued working, your benefits would continue for three more months and then be terminated. So, for me it was a quantum leap of faith. If this job didn't work out and my trial work period expired, then I would have to reapply for my Social Security benefits and start my search for employment all over again.

I could not believe that I was going to be working at the rehabilitation facility where I was a patient just three years before. I had no background in healthcare whatsoever but, hopefully, I could use my creativity and ask the right people for help and make this work. In doing an assessment of what the needs were at that time, there was a lot of misinformation regarding a new steroid protocol for newly injured persons that needed to be administered within eight hours of injury. After doing a lot of research, I only found one emergency room poster that had been done in Florida several years before. So, I thought, this was a good start.

Working with the staff at Shepherd Center, I created an emergency room poster that addressed the urgent care and treatment of persons that presented in the ER with a spinal cord injury and a post injury condition called Dysreflexia. Dysreflexia could be a life-threatening condition if not treated immediately. After several months of passing a draft of the poster around and soliciting feedback from the Shepherd Center staff, Dr. Apple added one last condition. The dermatome man on the poster needed to have a smile. I would affectionately call this the "Apple Grin". Working with Dawn Boyle in the marketing department, it took forever to put a smile on that silly man's face. Computer graphics software in the early 90s was very complex and difficult to work with.

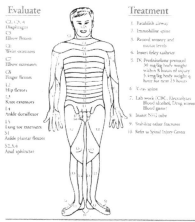

When it was all said and done, though, the poster was perfect. We distributed the posters to hospitals throughout the Southeast and they were well received.

Later we would take the poster and reduce it to a reference card size with the primary scene survey that was utilized by first responders on the back and added other helpful information. Those cards were distributed to paramedics and healthcare professionals.

Shortly thereafter, I started working with the Paralyzed Veterans Administration and the staff at Shepherd Center and embarked on creating a physician's manual on primary care for spinal cord injured persons. This manual was to be a vital resource for discharged patients returning home and was found to be useful in providing a reference book for primary care physicians.

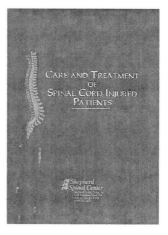

CHAPTER EIGHTEEN:
A Gift to Share with the World

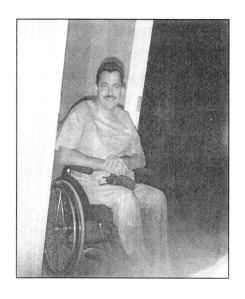

"I'm not a Doctor, but I did stay in a Holiday Inn Express once."
-Holiday Inn Commercial

June 28, 1993, was the day we received the gift of the birth of my daughter, Emily Cristine Miears. That "one in a million chance" came into this world as a healthy baby girl, the same child who wasn't to be possible without a lot of medical intervention and luck.

To quote that great philosopher, Lloyd from the movie, "Dumb and Dumber", "There's always a chance." In a scene at the beginning of the movie, Lloyd is a bumbling limousine driver and is taking a millionaire heiress to the airport. He's trying to have a chatty conversation with her and believes that things between them are going great. After he drops her off at the airport he asks for a hug and then says, "So do you think there's a chance that I can see you again", and she replies, "Chances are probably just one in a million", Lloyd is excited and exclaims, "Great, so you are saying there's a chance?" However great the odds, there's always a chance.

Emily was a testament that all things are possible regardless of the odds; a one in a million chance is always a chance worth taking.

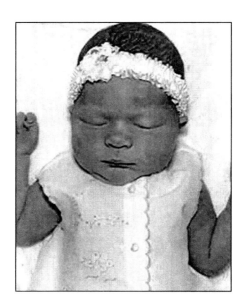

CHAPTER NINETEEN:
Employment:
The Final Frontier

"Do not lose hold of your dreams or aspirations. For if you do, you may still exist but you have ceased to live."
- Henry David Thoreau

Ever since my injury, I had longed for the day that I would once again be gainfully employed. In June, 1993, I applied for a new position that was being created in the marketing department at Shepherd Center. This position would be their first external full-time marketing position. I put my best suit on and went to interview with Vicki Miller, who was the Director of Clinical Evaluators. I wasn't sure what my competition was for the position, but I felt that I had impressed everyone with my accomplishments in my current position and past experience and was worthy of consideration. Plus, I had something that no one else had, I was a past patient and what better example of their program than to have me representing Shepherd Center.

I did get the position and became Shepherd Center's first full-time marketer.

This was amazing. The rehab facility where I was a patient just three years earlier, where I often stared up at the ceiling in my room for hours wondering what kind of life and work could I possibly find moving forward, had put me here.

I had found very meaningful work and had returned full-time to the workforce. In a million years, I never would've thought that I would've been working at Shepherd Center. I remember the meeting with Betsy Fox, the Director of Human Resources, who went over all of the benefits that I would receive as a full-time employee. I was elated and so was my family. All of the decisions and the effort I made to regain my financial independence from Social Security along with all of the support I received, I had made it, I had made it!

In my new position, my primary responsibility was to call on referring hospital case managers and social workers and share with them the benefits Shepherd Center could offer their spinal cord injured patients who were in need of rehabilitation. I was honored to take on this role, because what better testament to the program's success than to have one of its former patients in one of the most visible roles the hospital had?

When I would meet with potential patients and their families at referring hospitals, they were often amazed that I was there, that I had driven or flown there and had rented a car to get to the hospital – that things like that are possible. In some way, maybe they could see some hope, life could get better, and there could be some sense of normalcy that could return to their lives. I wasn't there to tell them that their loved one would be in a wheelchair the rest of his life. I was there to tell them that there was still a meaningful and productive life even if you were in a wheelchair.

In December of 1993, some changes took place in the Admissions and Clinical Evaluator Departments. Both Admissions and Clinical Evaluator Directors were leaving. James Collins, who was the CEO of Shepherd Center, had moved on and Jason Shelnutt the CFO was now acting as the interim CEO of Shepherd Center while the search was on to find Mr. Collins' replacement.

I was asked to consider taking the director position of the now merged Admissions and Clinical Evaluator Departments. I didn't believe I was prepared to serve in that position, since I had never done anything like that before. But, I understood. Shepherd Center relied on referrals to come into the hospital to generate patients and I saw my responsibility to make sure that the phone would ring and that the response would be as appropriate as possible for an admission to occur.

Here I was, now the Director of Admissions for the largest Spinal Cord Rehab Hospital in the world. I was having lunch with Dr. Apple shortly after the announcement had been made to the Board of Directors. Dr. Apple said, "Wow, three jobs in less than one year, that's incredible, what's next?" So I jokingly said, "Dr. Apple, what exactly do you do around here?" My mom did want me to be a doctor.

During that time, I still had some marketing responsibilities, but I had suggested Robert Antonisse as my marketing replacement. Robert, my peer supporter while I was a patient at Shepherd Center, had been living; breathing proof of what everyone had told me was possible. He was working with Travelers Insurance at the time and was showing me pictures from a recent trip he had taken to Hawaii. After meeting with him, I started to believe that I was bigger than my accident and that I could do something meaningful with my life. He inspired me to push myself and become more than I thought was initially possible. What better replacement for me than another successful previous patient?

As the new Director of Admissions, my challenges were many. First, I needed to earn the respect of the admissions and clinical evaluators in the department. Secondly, I needed to gain the respect of the doctors and nurses in the hospital. This would certainly take some time. I believed my role was to primarily make sure the staff in the department had the resources they needed to do their job and to work as efficiently as possible and to get patients into the hospital. This was certainly a work in progress and would take months for me to feel comfortable in my role.

My wife and I went to our first Shepherd Center Legendary Ball that year. It's an annual Black Tie fundraiser devoted to raising awareness and financial needs of programs and services often not funded by insurance. She does make me look good.

CHAPTER TWENTY:
Opportunities to Do Something about It

"One way to get the most out of life is to look upon it as an adventure."
- William Feather

One of the concerns I had while working in the admissions department was that the gurney used by paramedics to transport patients to Shepherd Center and anywhere else had not changed in over 20 years. The gurney itself had a high density foam mattress on the top which was designed more for durability than comfort. Shortly after a spinal cord injury, you lose muscle mass and sensation and are more susceptible to skin breakdown.

Many patients must often travel hundreds of miles by ground ambulance from other hospitals to receive rehabilitation at Shepherd and this trip can be traumatic to the patient's skin. Working with Lee Anderson of Jay Mattress and Jeff Sussman with Metro Ambulance, we created a special ambulance. The Jay Mattress was a pressure relief mattress designed to reduce skin breakdown. Metro Ambulance provided a mobile intensive care unit staffed with health professionals who were trained in the care of persons with a spinal cord injury. Additionally, the ambulance provided room for up to four family members compared to a conventional ambulance that had room for only one or two family members to travel with their loved one to Shepherd Center.

A One-of-a-Kind Ambulance

Shepherd Center is a specialty hospital. So it seems only natural that patients who are brought here need a specialty ambulance.

Now, through the efforts of Shepherd, Metro Ambulance, Jay Mattress and Ferno, a division of Ferno Washington, a unique ambulance has been designed to meet the particular needs of people with spinal cord injuries.

This unique vehicle has a special pressure relief mattress to reduce skin breakdown in people who are paralyzed. Many patients must travel hundreds of miles by ambulance from other hospitals to receive rehabilitation at Shepherd and this trip can be traumatic to the patient's skin.

continue functioning under almost any condition. The ambulance provides room for up to four family members to ride along in the front cab as compared to a conventional ambulance, with room for only one or two family members. In addition, it is staffed with health professionals who specialize in spinal cord injury.

Based in Atlanta, the ambulance can retrieve patients from hospitals throughout the Southeast, within a 400-mile radius. What's more, the charge for this specialized ambulance is no more than that for a regular ambulance. Shepherd can also provide a nurse to support the ambulance staff depending on the condition and needs of the

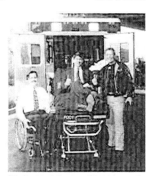

Giving thumbs up to the new specialty ambulance are (l to r) Dan Miears of Shepherd Center, Lee Anderson of Jay Mattress and Jeff Sussman of Metro Ambulance.

An article on the, "One-of-a-Kind Ambulance" was included in the Shepherd Spinal Column magazine.

Overall, the ambulance was a great success. We had some issues with the weight of the J mattress and referring hospitals allowing us to send an ambulance from Atlanta to pick up their patient. We did prove that, just as

Shepherd Center is a specialty hospital, the use of a specialty ambulance was beneficial in maintaining the patient's health while in route to our facility. I developed a deep respect for the people I worked with and the patients and families we brought into the center.

I also realized that a nurse was needed in the admissions department to assist with getting approval from the insurance companies for our services. I added Marilyn Taylor, a long-time Shepherd employee to the department. I had hopes that she would, one day, replace me as I aspired to continue growing professionally at Shepherd Center.

During my time as the Admissions Director, admissions to Shepherd Center grew by 20%. I believe that I was in the right place at the right time during this period of transition waiting for the arrival of a new CEO and Vice President of Marketing. Shortly after the arrival of Mitch Fillhaber, the new VP of Marketing, I returned to the Marketing Department. I told Marilyn Taylor that the department was now all hers. She had earned it and I was very pleased to be passing it off to her very capable hands.

In 1997, I made the decision to go back to college and complete my degree. I had stopped going to Georgia State after I started working full-time. I decided to finish at Shorter College and in 1999 received a Bachelor of Science in Business Administration degree. Working full-time and going to school at night was very taxing on me and my family. But this was very important for me; to finish something that I started and, for my children, to see that you can accomplish anything you set your mind to.

One of the great mentors I've had in my professional career is Mitch Fillhaber. Mitch always seemed to have

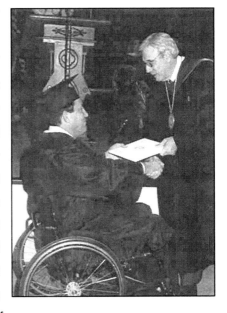

the right answer or perspective for a situation and would be the ideal first responder to calm down any situation and bring the parties together to get to a solution. Mitch, takes the Swiss approach, and tries to be friends with everyone. I have learned a lot working with Mitch and still count on him as a guru from time to time on issues regarding healthcare and life.

During my time at Shepherd Center I had the opportunity to participate in various activities. One was being the host of the annual talent show. The first year I went as President Bill Clinton. He had recently fallen down the steps at Greg Norman's house in Florida and needed to be in a wheelchair for several weeks while he recuperated from his injures. I went to the seating clinic and borrowed a wheelchair with the right leg extended out. I did a pretty good impression of his voice and was a big hit. Since that day, Harold Shepherd has always called me, "Mr. President".

I worked in the marketing department in various roles until spring of 2006. There were so many great people that I had the opportunity to work with at Shepherd Center and at the referring hospitals I got to know over the years. I am truly honored and blessed to have had the opportunity to get to know and work with each of them.

One of those was Kathy Adams, a clinical evaluator I worked with in Tennessee and Alabama. Kathy is one of the most unique people that I have ever met. There are people that you meet that have an aura that draws you in and Kathy is one of those people. Kathy always has an upbeat attitude regardless of the challenges the day may bring. Kathy and I were very successful in building new relationships with hospitals we worked with in Chattanooga, Tennessee and Huntsville, Alabama. Kathy has an incredible story in her own right and I hope one day that she will take the time to write a book. Her life story would make a great Hallmark movie.

Kathy Slonaker, another clinical evaluator for Shepherd Center that I worked with in Central and South Georgia and North Florida, was probably born to work at Shepherd Center. She has been there almost from the beginning and her passion for the patients and their families is amazing. We traveled more like two friends, talking about raising our children and the challenges of life we faced.

There was one time working with Kathy Slonaker that I will never forget. Kathy and I were doing presentations on Spinal Cord Injury, "The First 72 Hours" for the nurses in the Intensive Care Unit at Shands-Jacksonville Hospital in

Jacksonville, Florida. Taking a break, we decided to go down to the coffee shop and get some caffeine and a snack. It was very crowded and the only place left to sit, was at the end of one of the partially occupied tables. There was an elderly couple sitting there and we asked if we could join them. They said, "OK", and we joined them and started a light hearted conversation. I noticed that he was wearing a patient bracelet, and asked, "Are you here as a patient?" He said, "Yes, this is my last chance to get rid of this cancer." And then, almost without hesitation, he reached over and grabbed his wife's hand and said, "And I'm going to live until I die!" Wow! We were not expecting to see or hear that. They both had such a glow about them, you could tell they were truly in love and cared so much for each other.

It was an epiphany for me. I am going to enjoy my life, whatever it is. Walking, rolling or crawling, I am going to live until I die. We were both so touched by them and I have thought back, numerous times, to that day and, have mentioned them from time to time during my presentations.

There were so many wonderful evaluators I had the opportunity to work with, Sharon Kirby, Tina Jarrard, Dorea Fowler, Susan Lawhorn, Linda Faber, Cheryl Brown and Jenny Mitchell. They are all incredible!

In 1995, Shepherd Spinal Center changed its name to Shepherd Center when they opened a 20-bed unit for people with brain injuries. In 1997 the Center added Shepherd Pathways, a residential rehabilitation facility in neighboring Decatur to provide community-based outpatient services and a day program for ABI patients.

I wish that program had been in place when I had my injury. I could have moved to Shepherd Center earlier and avoided some of the setbacks I encountered.

CHAPTER TWENTY-ONE:
I'm No Actor

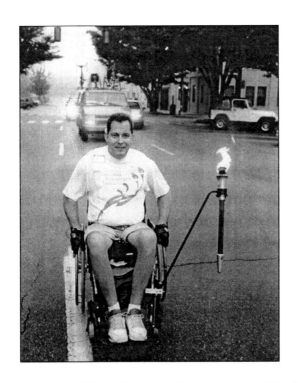

*"Only those who risk going too far can possibly find out
how far they can go."*
- T.S Eliot

In 1996, I had the opportunity to have several life experiences. One was to carry the Paralympics torch as it made its way to Atlanta. The other was to be in a made-for- TV movie that was partially being filmed at Shepherd Center, "A Step Toward Tomorrow". The movie starred Judith Light, who portrayed a single mother whose son had suffered a spinal cord injury. The premise of the movie was her HMO insurance company wouldn't pay for a spine stimulator to help her son with his severe spasticity and portrayed her struggle to get it paid for and the challenge of her two sons in dealing with how the injury occurred.

Additionally, Christopher Reeve had a cameo role in the movie as one of the patients in the rehabilitation hospital. On the night before filming, Christopher had served as the Master of Ceremonies for opening night of the Paralympics Games being held in Atlanta. There were three scenes that were to be filmed at Shepherd Center. Several other employees and I had been selected as extras for the movie and were anxiously waiting our turn in the Shepherd Center auditorium.

What I found out about movie extras is they feed you well and don't pay you much. We were to receive $50 for the day less $10 for our membership into the Screen Actors Guild. Yes, I became a card-carrying member of the Screen Actors Guild and all that entitled me to.

The director of the movie approached me and told me to follow her as they were setting up one of the scenes. Upon arriving there, she handed me a piece of paper and said, *"Practice reading these lines."* Shortly thereafter, Judith Light came in and asked, *"Are you ready to go over the lines?"* I said, *"Suuure."* She already knew her lines, which I thought was totally unfair. I tried my best to read my lines and realized at that point that I am no actor.

Judith was very gracious and we bantered back and forth for several minutes going over each of our lines. Christopher came into the room and the director said that I could leave now. They were using me to set up the scene for Christopher, I guess, since I was either the tallest guy in a wheelchair,  resembled him or it was just plain luck. I was somewhat relieved and disappointed that I was essentially his stunt double/stand-in (ha ha). But, I really was okay with it. This took place again as the day went on with the other scenes. The one scene in the movie I am in is the scene in the gym. That's me off to the right of the mirror. At the end of the day, I still had not spoken directly to Christopher. As he and his wife, Dana, were heading back to the room he was using to take breaks in, I passed them and then turned around. I told Christopher, "Thank you, you are fighting a good fight for all of us." I'm not sure what made me choose those words but I wanted him to know I appreciated what he was doing on behalf of everyone with a spinal cord injury.

Christopher Reeve, Superman, put a face on spinal cord injury for humanity's sake. This was a beloved superhero character that had been felled by something greater than kryptonite and the world was pulling for him to regain his strength. There were no phone booths needed now to become Superman. He became a true Superman 24/7 for all of us.

> *"You are more than you are."*
> *– Christopher Reeve*

As James Shepherd's injury led to the creation of Shepherd Center, so did Christopher Reeve's injury lead to the creation of the Christopher and Dana Reeve Foundation. The Reeves now responded to the call, to assist others whose life journeys now resembled their own.

Marc Buoniconti, the son of Nick Buoniconti, sustained a spinal cord injury in 1985 during a Citadel football game. Father and son soon became animating forces for the University of Miami's fledgling Miami Project to Cure Paralysis. Scientists snickered at the audacity. Cure paralysis? Might as well try to cure death. But Nick leveraged his fame and his connections and Marc told his never-give-up story of hope; together they've raised roughly $350 million for the Buoniconti Fund, the fundraising arm of the Miami Project. (Source: USA Today 9/24/2010)

I have joked several times with James Shepherd about whether he knows it was his fault that Shepherd

Center is there? Think about that for a minute. Had James not had his accident, or had it been less severe, there never would have been a Shepherd Center or any place like it in Atlanta or anywhere else. There would have been no Shepherd Center for me to go to, or for the tens of thousands of people it has helped to restore hope and rebuild their lives over the years.

I do not wish a catastrophic injury on anyone. But think how different the world would be if these injuries had not occurred; James Shepherd, Christopher Reeve, Marc Buoniconti? They all have had a huge impact on so many lives. Not in spite of their injury but because of their injury, they have made the world a better place and the future one of hope for persons with spinal cord injuries.

I can honestly say that if I hadn't gone to Shepherd Center, I believe my life after my injury would have been much more difficult, with less opportunity, and much less of a positive outlook on my future.

Great deeds in life often don't occur by an accident but occur after the accident itself. I believe inherently, as humans, we want to make the path a little less painful for someone who is going through what we've been through. That is why, for example, you often see cancer survivors reaching out to people just diagnosed with cancer. They have been there, they know what it's like, and they are living, breathing proof that you can survive, you can get through it.

The Shepherd family, Christopher Reeve and many others are truly my heroes. For me, I want to be a hero for my wife, my children, and family. I want to be someone that they can look up to, maybe not with heroic efforts, but with a heroic heart in dealing with the daily challenges I face.

For me, it was to take on the adversity of life with my best effort. I wasn't as concerned with my family seeing me fail, as much as I was concerned with them not even seeing me try. You can be that same hero, too, for your family, regardless of the adversity you are faced with.

Golfing or Goofing Around

My golf game is both better and worse since my accident. I don't drive the ball as far, so I don't lose as many balls, but it takes a lot more time to set up for a shot. I did sink this 27 foot putt at the Heritage Club in Norcross. This turned out to be my best shot of the day.

CHAPTER TWENTY-TWO:
Time to Go

"I do not want to get to the end of my life and find that I just lived the length of it. I want to have lived the width of it as well."
- Diane Ackerman

I never thought I would work at Shepherd Center and I never thought that I would ever leave. However, I felt I had reached the potential of what I had to offer Shepherd Center and the time had come for me to, once again, challenge myself and consider looking for a new opportunity.

Over the years, I have met a lot of interesting people whose companies provide services to Shepherd Center patients. One such person was Rick Moore, President of Medway Air Ambulance. Rick had said several times, "I've got a place for you whenever you're ready." So here was an opportunity for me to go and do something different, to learn about the air ambulance industry first-hand and work closer to home. So I made the decision to leave Shepherd Center, a place that I truly love and will forever be indebted to for the gift I received from my rehabilitation there.

I went to work at Medway Air Ambulance and, as luck would have it, timing could've been better. Things started out okay, but then Rick, unfortunately, ran into some issues with the FAA regarding the leasing of his planes on another certificate. After several months of trying to resolve this issue, Rick was unsuccessful in coming to an agreement with them and Medway's planes were grounded until it could be worked out.

Rick did the best he could to keep everyone on the payroll. With all the challenges that Rick and Medway faced, I felt that it was in my best interest to look for another marketing position in the healthcare industry. I had learned a lot from Rick about the air ambulance industry and what it takes to move someone from across the state or the other side of the world.

Rick finally did resolve his issues with the FAA and received his own 1-35 Certificate. Way to go Rick!

CHAPTER TWENTY-THREE:
Life of a Dragonfly

"To fly with purpose, there is no higher honor."
– Dan Miears

I called up my dear friend, Kathy Adams, and asked her to mention my name to anyone she knew looking for a Director of Marketing. Kathy had left Shepherd Center in 1997. She and her husband, Steve, always had an entrepreneurial mindset and in October of 2001, they started Accord Services, a private duty nursing company for persons with spinal cord injuries in Georgia.

They started working out of their home and probably jokingly said, "Maybe we'll just have a couple clients and be able to stay at home and be with our boys."

Kathy chose the dragonfly as the company logo because of what it represented. It would become one of the most recognized company logos in the industry.

The meaning of a <u>dragonfly</u> changes with each culture. The main symbolisms of the dragonfly are renewal, positive force and the power of life in general. Dragonflies can also be a symbol of the sense of self that comes with maturity. Also, as a creature of the wind, the dragonfly

frequently represents change. And as a dragonfly lives a short life, it knows it must live its life to the fullest with the short time it has - which is a lesson for all of us.
(Source:www.answers.com)

Well, the company grew from that humble beginning and by 2003 they had outgrown the home office and moved to a larger office space on the square in Marietta. Kathy said during our conversation that it just so happened that they were currently interviewing for a Director of Marketing. After meeting with her and Steve, I was given the opportunity to come and work with them.

In August of 2006, I started my career at Accord Services. Over the years, Accord Services has grown to become a recognized leader in home care for catastrophic injured workers in Georgia. It is with great pride that I'm associated with the caring people that work at Accord Services who are of the highest integrity.

Integrity and trust is something that most people take for granted. I have often told my children that integrity is the greatest asset you can ever possess. Integrity means that you are a person of your word and that your word is truthful and honest. If you are without integrity you have nothing.

You can be the most talented person at what you do, but if you cannot be trusted, you have nothing! Once you give up your integrity, you will never be able to get it completely back. Integrity is something that I will always have with me regardless of where my travels in life take me.

CHAPTER TWENTY-FOUR:
I Roll with R&R Mobility

"No other man-made device since the shields and lances
of ancient knights fulfills a man's ego like an automobile."
— Lord Rootes

One night my wife and I were shopping in Publix Grocery store and she started to feel like she was having a heart attack. We rested for a couple of minutes to see if it would pass and I told her I was going to call the paramedics. She said to hold off and in a couple of minutes felt a little better and well enough to make it out to the car. When I was transferring into her car my right hand slipped off of my wheelchair and I felt one of the most excruciating pains in my life. Now, I have lived with a lot of pain since my injury, broken back, neck, shoulder etc., but this pain was epic. I had been having some pain in my right elbow and had received several steroid shots to alleviate the pain. I had several bone spurs that were aggravating at times. I had torn my right tricep tendon from my elbow. Wow that hurt. To make a long story short, my wife was diagnosed as having an anxiety attack. The day before she had been told that a mass had shown up on her mammogram. That's a scary word to have appear in your life. Fortunately, after a more detailed exam it proved to be a false alarm. For me though, I was going to need surgery and would be out of work for at least three months while I recovered.

During my break from working non-stop for almost 20 years, an opportunity for change in my life took place. I had enjoyed working for Accord Services for over seven years and the time came to do something different. After considering several consulting opportunities, I had the opportunity to work for R&R Mobility Vans and Lifts.

After almost 24 years since my accident, I was right back to a pivot point that had occurred earlier in my life. After I left Shepherd Center in 1990 I was waiting for my step mom's van to be modified by R&R Mobility Vans and Lifts. Thank God vocational rehabilitation was there to pay for the modifications that were needed so I could drive it. While I was waiting I was being driven around by my wife. Being dependent on her to take me where I needed and wanted to go reminded me of an earlier point in my life when I was a kid and a teenager being driven around to all school functions, going to the mall, movies etc. I couldn't wait to regain the most important of all of my independences, true mobility freedom, being able to go where and when I wanted to go, not dependent on anyone's schedule.

When the van was completed my dad drove me to R&R to pick it up. I felt like a giddy 16 year old all over again – the apprehensive butterflies, the exhilaration of regaining control of my life. This van was more than just transportation, it allowed me to drive to Georgia State University in the fall, it could take me anywhere and at the time, I truly felt like my life was back on track.

For me, R&R Mobility Vans and Lifts has felt like coming home. After all of my years working in rehabilitation and healthcare, it was the perfect opportunity for me to take everything I had learned and apply it at an incredible place. R&R, like Shepherd Center, was started by a family. They opened their doors May of 1974 because one of the founders' family members was in a wheelchair. In trying to get a Handicap Van to allow him to regain some mobility, they found the market in Georgia left little in the way of choices.

There were no dealers or manufacturers of wheelchair accessible or handicapped vans or lifts in Georgia at that time. Handicapped persons had very limited mobility because of this. Out of necessity they started their own Handicap Van facility in a garage in their back yard. They became the first Mobility Dealer in Georgia. Like many great companies that started in a garage, they continued to grow and have now become one of the largest single location dealers for vans and lifts in the country. Now celebrating their 40th Anniversary, I had an opportunity to become part of this great organization and share my sales and marketing expertise and help this company continue to grow.

Someone asked me, what it is like working at R&R. I said, "Well it's kind of like Duck Dynasty, a show on the A&E network, does vans and lifts. They are a family of hard working, gun toting, God fearing Americans who would do anything to help you." With some humor we take our work seriously and try to provide the best experience possible. Everyday people come in and get a van or lift from us. They work, they play, and they live their lives. We don't sell vans or lifts, we sell journeys. I am honored to be part of our customers feeling like that 16 year old for the first time or, like me, for a second time with butterflies in their stomachs and a yearning to be as independent as possible. In a way it is a Declaration of Independence, that now more than any other time in your life, you have the freedom and the responsibility to go where and when you want. Now the really tough decision, to focus on what you are going to do, once you get there!

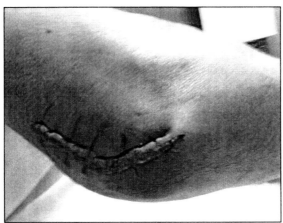

When I tore my right triceps tendon, I knew had to relinquish my independence during my recovery. Ray Lewis with the Baltimore Ravens had also torn his right triceps tendon. His projected recovery time was going to be twelve weeks as well. I did not have access to his resources but i was determined to make it back in 12 weeks myself. After surgery by the great Alan Pelchovic, I wore a cast for 4 weeks until my next visit when the cast was removed to check the progress and then another cast was put on. I literally became totally dependent on my wife and family for everything. Transfers in and out of bed into my wheelchair, bathing, going to the bathroom – you name it. This was a very challenging time for me; I had been totally independent with my life. My beautiful wife was getting worn out caring for me and working full time. My children helped and somehow we managed to get through it. Aging is more difficult as you get older, after almost 25 years of aging with a spinal cord injury it's hard to tell how much that impacts my body. Being one arm down even for just a couple of months opened my eyes to things wearing out, falling off, and not working the way they once did. I know moving forward I'm going to pay a lot more attention to what's going on and be more proactive in my health. and the decisions I make. I hope to never go through that again.

"Suffering is relative, if you're alive, it could be worse" - Amy Copeland

CHAPTER TWENTY-FIVE:
I Have Something to Say

"We have only this moment, sparkling like a star in our hand – and melting like a snowflake."
- Marie B. Ray

In 1994, I started speaking at several trauma and insurance conferences around the Southeast. I'm not sure what led me to want to get in front of people and tell my story, maybe as a way for me to hopefully inspire them keep doing what they do and let them know that they make a difference. Over the years, I have been very touched by the people that I've met. From first responders, to emergency room and intensive care unit staff, to therapists, nurses, adjusters and case managers who have made it their life's work to help

Photo courtesy of the Newnan Times-Herald

others. As Sherpas, they do genuinely care for the people who often come into their life as strangers and try to help them get better, regain their footing and reach for higher ground in their own "life's climb."

Over the years, I've been given the opportunity to speak to thousands of people at conferences throughout the United States. I've shared with them my personal journey of recovery and that of others who have inspired me. One of my most memorable presentations was speaking at the South Carolina Trauma Conference in 1994.

At the end of my presentation, I had a slide show of people I have known or heard of who had sustained catastrophic injuries like me and got on with their life. The slide show lasted about three minutes with Bette Midler's song, "Wind Beneath My Wings", playing in the background. It's a very touching tribute I gave to the attendees to let them know that although they may be unsung heroes, their work does not go unnoticed. In fact they are the wind beneath many people's wings helping them get to a higher place. At the conclusion of my presentation, a woman near the front row stood up and was crying. She said that she was going to go in to work later that day to resign, but that now, she was committed more than ever to working in the emergency room. I believe that I reaffirmed her purpose that she was doing angels' work.

For all of the paramedics, doctors, nurses, and other healthcare professionals who are part of emergent and trauma care who have chosen this as your life's work, I thank God, for you are "the wind beneath my wings," and the wings of many others.

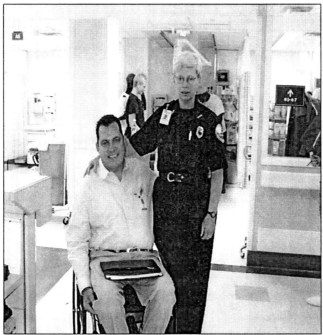

Here's me with one of my hero's, Mary Ann. When this picture was taken, she had retired as a paramedic and was doing dispatch at Northeast Georgia Medical Center,

CHAPTER TWENTY-SIX:
Are You Looking At Me?

"The fear of attention is not knowing what to do with it."
– Dan Miears

Getting Past the Obvious

It's not as important what people see as much as what they see me doing. My wheelchair is usually the first thing that people notice, my hope is that it's the last thing that they remember, and that's up to me.

I recall one time I was doing peer support with a 16-year-old patient at Shepherd Center. I was asking him about the night before when he and several other patients went to Lenox Square Mall to go shopping. I asked him how it went and he said, "it sucked, everywhere we went people just looked and stared at me." I said, "You've got it all wrong, people will go and spend tens of thousands of dollars just to get noticed. What you need to be thinking is now that you have their attention, what are you going to do with it?"

Unless some celebrity or someone else with a more obvious disability than yours is following you, you will usually always get everyone's attention first and that's not a bad thing.

I embrace the attention that my chair brings, not for sympathy or empathy or someone's pity, but the opportunity that it gives me to do something positive. At most of the conferences I have attended or presented at over the years, I am usually the only person there in a wheelchair or who has an obvious disability.

I once spoke at a disability conference with over 900 attendees. As I started my presentation, looking out at the audience, many in wheelchairs and scooters, I said to them, "the first word that comes to my mind as I look out and see you, is competition, because I'm used to having the whole room all to myself." My disability adds to my uniqueness, but it's not the only thing unique about me. It gives me the opportunity to stick out from the crowd. I love that.

Whatever is most obvious about you shouldn't be the main attraction. If that's all you wish to be known for, it will leave little else for people to remember you by. There are things about all of us we wish were different; to be more attractive, to weigh less, to have a different physical image than the one we have. You can change some of these things with plastic surgery, by working out more, and taking better care of yourself. It's been said that, "fish rot from the head first." If your thoughts aren't in the right place, regardless of how attractive your exterior may be, you will never be truly whole and happy as a human being.

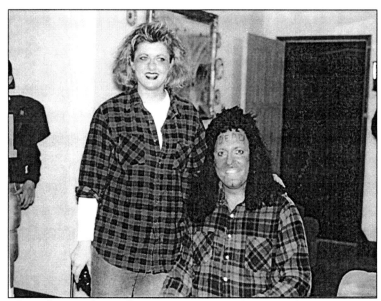

Dressing up for Halloween as a couple can always be an interesting result. We were Zombies one year. I am the taller one on the left. Just kidding, but you did look at the picture again to do a double check.

CHAPTER TWENTY-SEVEN:
The Road

"You are where you are today because of the decisions you have made thus far in your life."
- Neal Boortz

One of Life's little mysteries: why do you often find the possum dead in the middle the road? Ultimately, the possum died of indecision; it couldn't decide to continue crossing the road or to go back, so it was run over in the middle of the road. People often find themselves in the middle the road of life indecisive, not sure if they should continue on their journey or if they should go back. Be decisive and resolute in your decisions as you move forward in your life.

You see, "Life Is like a Big Game of Chicken," you versus whatever you're up against are always going to meet head-on and one of you will bail out each and every time. Life truly is a test of wills, you have to be steadfast and push through, whatever opposes you, get through it and keep moving forward. If what opposes me, takes me out, then I will have no regrets for staying the course and living my life to the fullest.

"Too many of us are not living our dreams because we are living our fears."
- Les Brown

For my wife's 40th Birthday Party, my neighbors and I had Harold Schultz, a great Elvis impressionist, perform for her on our deck by the pool. Needless to say, she is a big Elvis Fan.

CHAPTER TWENTY-EIGHT:
The Woods

*"Do not go where the path may lead, go instead
where there is no path and leave a trail."*
- Ralph Waldo Emerson

The woods can be an ominous and scary place. Many books and movies have been made about events that occur in and around the woods, from childhood favorites like "Little Red Riding Hood," to modern day horror films like "The Blair Witch Project."

In the woods there are often few paths and no signs of direction. Many people avoid the woods for fear of getting lost. There are only two types of people you will ever find in the woods, one is an explorer and the other is lost.

The explorer is looking for adventure or discovery; there's a sense of excitement as he moves through the woods. The person who is lost is looking for shelter, the way out, or for someone to save him; he has a constant sense of fear and panic.

We are not hardwired to be complacent. It's in our DNA to be explorers, to conquer what we do not know or understand.

We all live in the woods. Which one are you? Are you the explorer or are you the person that's lost. Your life is a lot like the woods and you have to decide: are you going to look for the excitement of the unknown, or are you always going to be fearful of what's around the next corner?

In life you will always be given the opportunity to choose a beaten-down path or a path less traveled. As inviting as the beaten down path looks, there is little, if anything, to be gained other than the certainty of the travels of others. We're often tempted by the easy path, because there is less risk of failure and there is safety in the knowledge that others have gone before us.

The path less traveled has been written about numerous times and is where you will find the explorers. They explore while gaining from the knowledge of others, content to pursue their own dreams, and they thrive on the adrenaline of the unknown and being the first to see what is around the corner.

CHAPTER TWENTY-NINE:
You Gotta Have Faith

*"I don't know what your religious faith is, but when
I meet my maker I don't want to have
to apologize for a squandered life."*
– Mark Partridge

Religious faith plays an important role in most people's lives. Regardless of your religious doctrine, there is belief of a higher being. I am a quiet, religious man who believes in God and that there is something greater that is beyond this world we live in. I'm not sure if there was divine intervention at play on the day that I had my accident.

I clearly was not expected to live by those who came in contact with me in the minutes, hours, and days that followed. I'm grateful for everyone who assisted in taking care of me and believe they are God's angels at work.

Over the years, I have met numerous people who were not expected to survive the horrific events that occurred in their lives. Even though their outcomes looked dismal, they survived those events. Sometimes the doctors and nurses had no explanation other than a higher power at work. They say the Lord works in mysterious ways. If he had a hand in my surviving my accident, then there must have been some deed or contribution I had yet to fulfill. I doubt I will ever know what that is until we meet.

I know this, as Mark said, the last thing that I want to do is to have to explain how I squandered my life. Whatever life this is, it's mine to live and I want to make the most of it. I hope that as you look at your life you embrace living it to the fullest.

> *"God may have taken my legs but he*
> *gave me the wings of imagination."*
> **– Pano Santos**

Cipriano (Pano) Santos was recently being interviewed on CNN; Pano is a senior scientist for Hewlett Packer and has been named one of the 50 most influential Hispanics in technology and business in the United States by the publishers of the Hispanic Engineer and Information Technology magazine. Born in Mexico City, Santos contracted polio at the age of three. Although physically stricken by this dreadful disease, he discovered that he had a true love and passion for physics and mathematics; he obtained his Master's degree and PhD in operations research at the University of Waterloo in Canada.

I'm always inspired hearing about people like Pano whose physical limitations were a catalyst to move him to a higher ground of discovery that so many benefit from on a daily basis.

One of the great pleasures of my life was coaching my daughter's basketball team at the Winder Barrow Recreational League for 5 years. The last year we went undefeated and made it to the state championship game and, sadly, lost to the home team. I was very proud of all of the girls on the team. Emily went on to play competitively in high school. I sure miss those days.

CHAPTER THIRTY:
The Three Groups

*"Life is unjust and this is what makes it so beautiful.
Every day is a gift. Be brave and take hold of it."*
- Garrison Keillor

There are only three groups of people that you will see in your life. In the first group, regardless of what resources they are given and help they receive, nothing will ever change in their lives. They are content to live their lives as a victim. They are always blaming events and others around them for their misfortune. Recently, we have seen this group get much larger due to the downturn in the economy. People have become much more dependent on the federal government to provide for their daily needs. I'm not against giving people a hand up, but I believe that we have begun to fund lifestyles of complacency that foster greater dependency and support of federal resources.

The entrepreneurial spirit that made America the most successful country in the world has slowly eroded over time as more and more people have become complacent and given up on pursuing their dreams. I truly believe that we each have something unique and valuable to contribute to this world we live in. I don't know how else to say this, but if you find yourself in this group, it is doubtful there will ever be a change in your life, because you will always look to place the blame somewhere else. You cannot go through life without having to face hardships that challenge all of us from time to time. As devastating as these events may be, you're still alive, you still have decisions to make and you still have to find the resolve to never give up.

In the second group, regardless of what they receive or not in life, they are going to be successful. You could give them a spoon and throw them out into the middle of the desert and they would be able to build a castle. They are not swayed by misfortune but are motivated by the opportunities they are given and never, ever give up on their dreams.

Last, there's a large group in the middle and they can go either way. Depending on how they react or respond to events in their life, take advantage of resources and support they are given, they will, ultimately determine their success or failure. They're trying to recover from a life-changing event and although uncertain of what the future holds, they have hope that things will get better and know for that to occur it will take everything they have to regain their footing and look for higher ground.

Which group are you in? Are you in the first group that will always live your life as a victim, take the easy path, and then complain about your lot in life? Or will you embrace the resources you have available to you and make the most out of how you react to changes in your life. Again, the choice is yours to make. You are not placed in one of these groups by someone else; you put yourself in the group of your choosing. You're not stuck in that group but you have to honestly look at yourself and say, "Is this really where I want to be?" If that's not really where you want to be in your life then you have to make a change in how you see and confront the challenges that you face on a daily basis.

We were not put on this earth to be spectators. We are here to add something of value to the world we live in. I hope that you are able to overcome whatever your limitations or obstacles are, and let the triumph of the human spirit take you far beyond what you believe is possible.

Conan O'Brien might have said it best in the closing remarks during his last night as host of *The Tonight Show*. He said, "Life is hard, it rarely turns out the way you planned, but if you work hard and you're nice to everyone, good things will happen for you."

If you cannot find work, volunteer, be part of something. There are numerous opportunities in the community you live in. Volunteering led to my first job at Shepherd Center. Over the years I have had the opportunity to be part of several meaningful organizations and committees.

I have served on Board of Directors for The Brain Injury Association of Georgia, a non–profit organization dedicated to assisting families and brain injury survivors with resources and support and, People Making Progress, another wonderful non-profit organization in Tucker, GA for adults with developmental disabilities. I have also served on the Board and as President of the Professional Rehabilitation Specialists of Georgia, a professional organization for case managers and rehab counselors. I was also honored to serve on the Georgia Trauma Advisory Committee, and currently serve on the Georgia State Board of Workers Compensation Advisory Committee.

CHAPTER THIRTY-ONE:
Relationships

"We laughed until we had to cry, we loved right down to our last goodbye, but over the years we'll smile and recall for just one moment, we had it all."
– Author unknown

Relationships in life are our most coveted possessions. The effort and energy expended on them sometimes leaves us exhausted and spent. They constantly recharge or deplete your batteries and fill you full of emotion. Being alone in life gives us no one to share the joys of life with and lean on when sorrow or loss fills our day.

I have sadly let some relationships slip away over the years, those of close friends and family, by not giving them the attention they deserve. At times in my life, I was content to go through life more as a loner, not believing that I needed to express how I cared or needed the comfort of others. I'm not one to pick up the phone and reach out to those I care about. Maybe it's a just a guy thing. It's not an excuse, though, and I continually try to improve on this major flaw of character and reach out now more than I ever have. The older you get, the more time becomes compressed. You find that you have less and less time and the years start to fly by. You have today, tomorrow is not promised to anyone. I may not have tomorrow for what I need to say today!

I have often said, "I'm a man living in a woman's world, the only difference between me and most men is that I know that." Knowing that, I have begun to truly understand the difference between empty words and caring words when expressing my love for those around me.

As we see the lives of others pass, we know one day our life will pass with no time left in the day. There will be no time to reach out to someone we care about and let them know how much we appreciate and care about them and what they mean to us.

My wife and I recently celebrated our 25th wedding anniversary. We have shared in many life changes that have come our way. We have gone through my injury together and started a new and different life that it gave us. We have celebrated the joy of bringing two wonderful children into this world. We have also felt the loss of friends and family over the years. Together we have gone through much.

If you are lucky, you recognize the joy of having someone by your side to share your "Life's Climb" with. To my beautiful wife, I say thank you. Thank you for being there with me to share in all of these things. Someone recently asked me, "Dan, Wow, 25 years how did you do it?" As I stated earlier in book, I had to be someone that she wanted to be with. For that matter, I had to be someone that my friends wanted to be with, and that my employer wanted to have working for them. I have developed many wonderful relationships over the years and I'm honored to have each and every one of them.

As far as staying married goes, it's very simple. You can be right, or you can be happy. But you can't be both right and happy. I have been right a couple of times in our relationship and those have been two of the most miserable nights of my life. I was actually right a third time, but I didn't tell my wife. And if I ever want to know what kind of day I'm going to have, I read my wife's horoscope. Fortunately, until now, she hasn't caught on yet, because we both have the same horoscope.

Some of my Danism's:

"My wife doesn't ever have to worry about me walking out on her."

I told her that I would never stand in her way."

I'm not disabled, but I have it on good authority the man that my wife sleeps with is."

"No one will ever accuse me of stepping out of line."

"Don't tell me to just walk it off."

"I'm about ready to recommend taking the warning labels off of everything and letting the laws of natural selection takes its course"

"I tried to minimize the wheelchair once by wearing bright colors. I turned out looking like a traffic cone with wheels."

Crissie and I all dressed up for a Luau Party

CHAPTER THIRTY-TWO:
Anchors Aweigh

"A ship in port is safe; but that is not what ships are built for. Sail out to sea and do new things."
-Rear Admiral Grace Hopper

We are all vessels of discovery. We were not put on this earth to take what is given to us, but instead find what is available to us. As you set out to sea on your life's journey, you need to assess the contents of your vessel and decide what is needed and what is not. I like to call these your anchors and oars. Some people and things are like an anchor that may keep us stuck in the past or present and unable to move forward with life.

Other people and possessions are like oars that empower us and allow us to move forward. Assess the anchors and oars in your own life and, if at all possible, cut your anchors loose, and if you can't cut them loose get them on board, so as not to slow you down. You're the captain of your own ship and, although you may be swayed by currents and winds beyond your control, it is your hand that is on the rudder. A ship will move much faster with oars going the same direction and distributed evenly. Look at your oars and where they are in your life and make sure that they are placed where they need to be.

As captain of your vessel, I hope you gather many oars in your journey of discovery. I also hope that you see yourself as an oar for many other vessels that you come across in your travels. We all need help from time to time and, like Sherpas, we benefit greatly from helping others get to higher ground.

> *"You can't pull someone up without also having pulled yourself up."*
> **- Zig Ziegler**

As you may learn, there are stowaways that find their way on to your vessel from time to time. In absence of a vessel of discovery of their own, they are content to go wherever you are going and, in a sense, are "along for the ride," finding great comfort in not having the responsibility of their own destination in life.

Just like in the movies, you will also have pirates show up from time to time, trying to take from you the treasures you have picked up along the way. These treasures can be many things from possessions to relationships of family and friends.

The sea, like the woods, can be a scary and ominous place. Sometimes, events occur in our lives like hurricanes and take us off course or, even worse, throw us onshore onto uncharted islands. I'm not talking about three-hour tours with Gilligan but deserted islands with little, if any, of the comforts we are used to.

There are so many wonderful life metaphors in movies and one of my favorites is from the movie, "Castaway". Chuck, played by Tom Hanks, had been rescued and had returned to Memphis where he had discovered that a funeral had been held for him and that his wife had gone on to marry someone else.

From the movie:

"We both had done the math. Kelly added it all up, knew she had to let me go. I added it up, knew that I had... lost her. Cause I was never going to get off that island. I was going to die there, totally alone. I mean I was going to get sick, or get injured or something. The one choice I had, the only thing I could control was when, and how, and where that was going to happen. So... I made a rope and went up to the summit, to hang myself. I had to test it, you know? Of course. You know me. In the weight of the log, snapped the limb of the tree. So I... I...I couldn't even kill myself the way I wanted to. I had power over nothing. That's when this feeling came over me like a warm blanket. I knew, somehow that I had to stay alive. Somehow, I had to keep breathing. Even though there was no reason to hope. And all my logic said that I would never see this place again. So that's what I did. I stayed alive. I kept breathing. And one day that logic was proven to be all wrong because the tide came in and gave me a sail. And now, here I am. I'm back. Insrega

Memphis, talking to you. I have ice in my glass. And I've lost her all over again. I'm so sad that I don't have Kelly. But I'm so grateful that she was with me on that island. And I know what I have to do now. I gotta keep breathing, because tomorrow the sun will rise and who knows what the tide could bring."

My take away from the movie is this. You can go back and rethink and replay past events in your life to hope the future will be different. At times when it looks like all is lost and there is nothing more to hope for, keep breathing, because tomorrow the sun will rise and who knows what the day could bring in.

CHAPTER THIRTY-THREE:
The Pain Game

*"Something new hurts every day; fortunately,
I don't remember what hurt yesterday."*
- Dan Miears

If you have lived your life at all, you have endured both emotional and physical pain. That's life.

In my accident, I broke my neck, my back, my right shoulder, my right hip, my right clavicle, and my face. I tried numerous medications to eliminate the pain. The best I could do was dull the pain and be fuzzy from the side effects of the medication. After the last medication I tried that was unsuccessful in eliminating the pain, I said enough was enough. I didn't want to have to deal with the side effects, much less become addicted to the medications. I didn't want to become reliant on the numbing sensation of the medication to dull the pain and make me so mentally numb to everything else in my life. I would rather be alive with my pain than fuzzy and numb with less pain. I would just work through it.

Research has shown that the more active you are, the less likely you will think about your pain. The more active I am, the less I focus on the pain from my injuries. I believe the best you can do is to make the pain more tolerable by focusing on other things. I discovered the more active I am mentally and physically, the less I focus on my pain. I do, from time to time, take over-the-counter pain medicines, use back massagers, stretch out on the bed, when the pain becomes a focus point of my attention and distracts me from the task at hand. I have also had some success with pain relieving creams and other homeopathic remedies. Living hurts less when you are moving. MOVE!

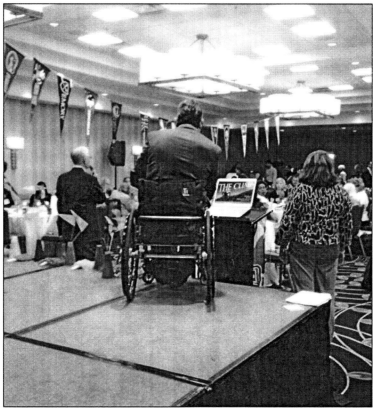

Here I'm getting ready to give my presentation at the 2012 Georgia State Board of Workers Compensation 2012 conference. My wheelchair doesn't make my butt look too big, does it?

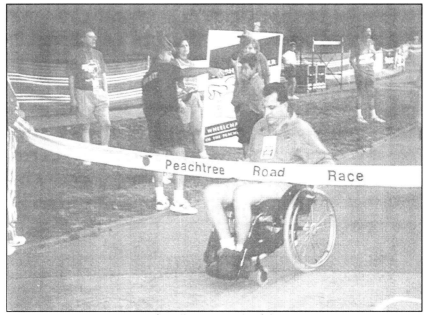

Being the opportunist

One time at the Atlanta Peachtree Road Race (the largest 5K road race in the world) I was asked to practice breaking the Finish Line tape. They wanted to make sure it would not decapitate the wheelchair winner as he crossed the finish line. I said I would do it under one condition, that you take a picture of me breaking the tape. I knew that would be the only time I would ever have a chance to do such a thing.

CHAPTER THIRTY-FOUR:
The Bottom Line

"Be careful. You will always find what you're looking for."
- Oliana Portnoy

The bottom line is, "are you looking for the way to accomplish something, or are you looking for the way out of having to do it?" Regardless of which one you choose, one thing is for certain: excuses are lies birthed by fear! We lie because we're afraid to accept responsibility for our own desires, abilities, or priorities. I'm afraid of hurting your feelings. I'm afraid of losing my job. I'm afraid of what you'll think of me. Facing the enemy, acknowledging the reasons, avoiding the excuses – those require the courage to confront our fears and refuse to allow them to control us. Easy to say, not so easy to do.

"Of all the liars in the world,
sometimes the worst are your fears."
- Rudyard Kipling

If you are always looking for the excuse to get out of something, then you will never really accomplish anything but blame and have numerous excuses for the failures in your life.

There's an old Native American story I heard that goes something like this: A wise old medicine man was teaching his pupil about the world, and he explained that every man has two coyotes living inside of him that are constantly doing battle. One is good, kind, and loving, and the other one is cruel, bad, and mean spirited. The student asked the old man, "Which one wins?" The old man's answer was: "The one you feed!" Which one of the coyotes are you feeding?

Remember that many of the choices you make that require the least effort also have the least reward. People who choose this path of life I call minimalist. They go through life doing as little as possible but surprisingly think they are due something for just showing up. I have always tried to exceed expectations, work a little harder than expected, learn a little more, and stay later, if needed, to get the job done. Pay more attention to the people that work around you and notice their work ethics. If they are working a little harder and surfing the internet less than others, seem to work later from time to time and always seem to know something new or have ideas to make things better, then they are probably going to be more successful than those around them.

If you're using events that have occurred in your life as an excuse for not being able to do things, what was your excuse before those events occurred? The mental barriers that you put before you every day are the greatest paralysis you will ever have. People often talk themselves out of doing something before they even try. The fear of failure keeps most people from discovering what their real capabilities are, what talents they have and what they are most passionate about.

One of my great honors was escorting Emily onto the football field for Homecoming Court her senior year.

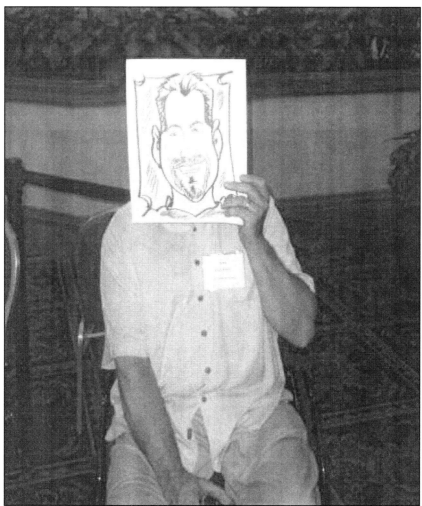

Are you the same person behind the veneer or façade that everyone sees? For me, whatever veneer I had before my injury was peeled away exposing the real me. I cannot pretend to be who I am not. What you see is what you get. Can the same be said of you? Are you pretending to be someone else?

CHAPTER THIRTY-FIVE:
It's A Wonderful Life

"Strange, isn't it? Each man's life touches so many
others. When he isn't around he leaves
an awful hole, doesn't he?"
- Clarence, George Bailey's guardian angel

My favorite movie of all time is, "It's a Wonderful Life". I love the premise of the movie, the principle character is granted his wish, "I wish I had never been born". George Bailey is given a tremendous gift, the opportunity to see how different the world would be like without him. He wasn't there to save his brother when he fell through the ice, Mr. Potter takes over the Building and Loan, his wife never gets married, so his four children are never born, and so many other events never took place, because he wasn't there.

For me, my family and friends who knew me before September 8, 1989, we have been given the opportunity to see how different things are, because I survived my accident, even though by all accounts I shouldn't have.

The events and contributions that I have shared in here would have never taken place. Everything past the date on the roadside memorial would not have been written because there was nothing to write. "Roadside memorials marking life's journeys never completed."

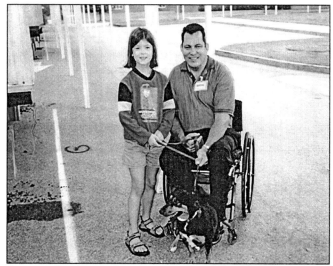

For me the best visual example of that is this picture.

It was pet day at Bramlett Elementary School. You know how you just go looking at a car with no intention of buying one. And what happens? You end up buying a car and taking it home. Well, one Saturday at 1:30 in the afternoon, we found ourselves at the Gwinnett County Animal Shelter. Shortly after arriving, an overhead announcement was made that they would be closing soon and if you were adopting an animal to finish your selection and come up to the front desk. I believe we must have heard that the building was on fire, and we needed to save at least one dog that day. Everyone scrambled to different areas of the building. After a couple of minutes, we heard Emily, "I found one, I found one".

We went over to where Emily was and she pointed to Angel, a Doberman Dachshund sort of dog that looked like it was covered in dust. I looked at my wife and said, "We are not getting a dog?"

So..., as we are filling out the paperwork, they gave Emily an Animal Shelter T-shirt. I said, "That's pretty cool, getting a T-Shirt for adopting an animal". The employee, said, "You may not have noticed it, but on Angel's cage was a yellow ribbon, today was the last day for her to be adopted!"

So for me, if it had not been for the heroes and Sherpas in my life, my dad, Mary Ann, Tyler, the medical staff at Northeast Georgia Medical Center, the picture would have looked like this that day.

The Parking lot would have been empty. I would not have survived my accident, my wife would have not had her husband, my son would have never known his dad, Emily would have never been born, and Angel would not have been saved that day.

**"Many lives' are eternally effected
by the events of just one accident"
– Art Berg**

You often don't know how things could have turned out if something different were to take place. For me, my life since September 8, 1989, has been, "A wonderful life" in reverse. I have been able to see what my life would have been. Yes Clarence, "It is a Wonderful Life".

CHAPTER THIRTY-SIX:
The Summit

"Life is not a journey to the grave with the intention of arriving safely in a pretty and well preserved body, but rather to skid in broadside, thoroughly used up, totally worn out, and loudly proclaiming – "WOW – What a Ride!"
-Anon

I can honestly say that if I didn't have my motorcycle accident my life would've not have been as rich and as rewarding. My injury put me on a new direction in life with higher elevation that demanded more of me than I thought I was possible or capable of. I have done more in my life than I ever could have imagined. I'm still climbing, and with the help of Sherpas around me, I'm constantly in search of higher ground.

The good news is that you don't have to go through a catastrophic event like I did to benefit from the lessons I have learned. You can take what I have shared with you in this book and apply it to your daily life. I hope that I have given you a higher elevation in life to aim for in your daily climb.

When my own life's climb is over, and is being looked at by my friends and family, I hope that it more resembles Mount Everest than Stone Mountain.

Which one will "The Climb of Your Life" look like when it's all said and done, and your friends and family look back on your life?

It's up to you, it always has been!

Keep Climbing!

EPILOGUE

Where are they now?

Dr. David F. Apple, Jr., served as Medical Director of Shepherd Center from the hospital's inception in 1975 until 2005, and now holds the position of Medical Director Emeritus.

That dashing Donald Peck Leslie, M.D. became the Medical Director of Shepherd Center in 2006. Prior to this appointment, he served for ten years as Associate Medical Director of Shepherd Center and Medical Director for Brain Injury Services.

Cheryl Linden, OT, is now a licensed professional counselor in the Spinal Cord Injury Rehabilitation Program at Shepherd Center, using her compassion and sense of humor to help patents and their families work through adjusting to the changes that have occurred in their lives.

Deborah Backus, Ph.D., PT, in 2012, became the director of research for the Andrew C. Carlos MS Institute at Shepherd Center. Deborah was previously the associate director of Spinal Cord Research, In 2004, she received her Ph.D. in neuroscience.

One of the PTs that kept up with me, Sarah Morrison, was named vice president of clinical services in 2012. Sarah is responsible for directing patient care, including

Shepherd's spinal cord injury, brain injury, chronic pain, and multiple sclerosis programs.

My primary nurse Carol Stephens retired from Shepherd Center several years ago.

Recently my mom gave me the fan that was in her mom's bedroom back in Texas. It's an Emerson fan from the 1940's and it still works. I guess we both have survived much in our lives.

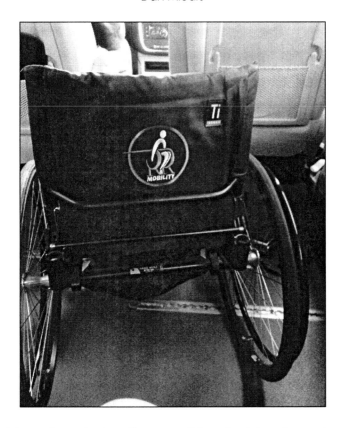

I need to acknowledge the one thing that has been beneath me for most of my important life's journeys since my injury, my TiLite© wheelchair. After having several wheelchairs after my rehabilitation at Shepherd Center, a revolutionary wheelchair came to the market; TiLite© in Pasco, Washington came out with a titanium frame wheelchair. This was epic for me, I have been pretty demanding of my wheelchairs, getting dressed in the mornings in them, traveling thousands of miles through the air and ground, and my first ones could not hold up to my hectic life. Then I received my first TiLite©, what a difference! We have gone on many a journey and I guess the best wheelchair is the one you don't have to think or worry about it holding up. The chair may not make the man, but this wheelchair has taken this man to all of the places I needed and wanted to go to without worry. Thank you TiLite© for getting me there!

CPSIA information can be obtained
at www.ICGtesting.com
Printed in the USA
FFOW05n1842031014